The Enchanted Soul

The Enchanted Soul

MARIA SHAW

Mid-Summers Eve Publishing
New Orleans, Louisiana

Believe in Angels
Believe in Fairies
Believe in Yourself
Become an Enchanted Soul!

For Jana and Sierra

CONTENTS

Contents

Contents

CHAPTER 19

Haunting Experiences

Reveals haunting tales and ghost stories that will make
you "a Believer".

CHAPTER 20

How to Live an Enchanted Life

Gives you practical hints for increasing your happiness
every day.

ACKNOWLEDGMENTS

I would like to thank God for giving me the time and talent to write and share my ideas with others. To the wonderful clients and friends I've met over the years who have supported me in many ways. To my parents and loved ones who have passed on but are still with me in spirit. To my great press agents in Los Angeles; Steve and Jarrett, for all of their hard work in getting our message out. To long-time buddies, Sharlotte, Jackie and Cindy, who have been through a lot of "stuff" with me. It's been great! To my dear friend Julie Newville, who handles all of my Florida appearances. And last, but not least, to my wonderful family who have sacrificed a lot so that I may do my life's calling. It's not easy living this crazy lifestyle, but I appreciate you and love you from the bottom my heart, David, Jana and Sierra.

INTRODUCTION

Since my last book, I didn't think I could possibly put together enough information to write another book so soon. But guess what? I started leaving notes all over my office, my kitchen table and even in my car . . . bits and pieces, fragments of ideas that I found interesting.

Since my first book, *Heart and Soul*, which was the culmination of my last 10 years as a relationship astrologer, I have begun some new journeys. I signed with a Los Angeles publicist who encouraged me to expand my lecture and seminar circuit. I've made appearances in major cities and smaller hubs, from Los Angeles to Ft. Lauderdale, Detroit to New Orleans and Minneapolis to Las Vegas.

Along the way, I've met some wonderful people. So many asked, "When is your next book coming out?" For a while I didn't have an answer or a clue. But I decided to begin writing what I teach at my seminars. I put together a list of the classes my clients enjoyed the most, and started from there.

This book, is filled with age-old wisdom, research I've done over the past 10 years and some enchanting stories. It's a combination of astrological and spiritual knowledge, ideas and design, that once you learn, will enhance your knowledge and improve your life!

As a professional astrologer I know these scientific theories, handed down over thousands of years by philosophers, gurus, religious leaders and common men (and women) have merit. Astrology has helped me improve my life and given me the opportunity to share this ancient wisdom with thousands of people, since 1990.

This book is not all about astrological studies, however. One of my most popular seminars is about working with energy. I've included that in this book too.

My purpose in writing *The Enchanted Soul* is to enlighten and brighten your world! I have written it out of love for the many people who have touched my life. Many of you I have been counseling for years. Some I have spoken with by telephone. Others have been guests on my radio shows. Thousands I have met briefly at new age expos and my Enchantment seminars, held around the country. And there are millions of you, I still anticipate meeting. So, with that said, please enjoy my gift to you!

Remember, love is the best gift you can give someone . . . it is also the best gift you can receive. Be open to all of your opportunities to share love.

Learn to create an enchanted life for yourself. Become an enchanted soul!

Keep peace in your heart!
Maria Shaw

ONE

Astrology and Life Cycles

★ ★ ★ Do you know that you have all of the answers to the mystery of life right above you? It is said, "Look to the Heavens" for your answers. Nothing could be closer to the truth.

Astrology is one the greatest tools we have to gain knowledge of our life's direction and path. Opportunity times and challenging periods can be pinpointed. Karmic patterns and your soul's spiritual purpose can also be found in an astrology or "birth" chart. This ancient science has proven to be reliable and accurate over the centuries.

Astrology explores the actions of the planets and stars in our solar system and how their movement influences us. An astrology chart reads like a road map of your life. It can tell you where you're likely headed. But remember, you're still driving the car!

To prepare a birth chart, all you need is your birth date, exact time of birth and the city in which you were born.

> **Maria's Tip:** In 1937, it became a Federal law to record the birth time of every baby born in the United States. Many people say they can't find their birth time and it isn't on their birth certificate. You need to contact the Office of Vital Statistics in the city in which you were born. There are two forms recorded in their office:
>
> 1. Notification of Birth, short form
> 2. Notification of Birth, long form
>
> You must request the long form with the time of birth on it.

An astrologer takes this information and designs a "wheel" divided into 12 equal sections. These sections are called "houses"; each represents an area of your life. For example, the second house has to do with money. Your fourth house holds home and family information. The tenth house contains knowledge about your career.

The planets were in certain positions at the exact moment you were born. They interacted with other planets in either positive or challenging ways. An astrologer can determine, based on the positions of these planets at your birth, what your personality and life may be like. When planets make "transits" (move from a current position in the sky), they connect with your birth planets in some way. Knowing *how* they can connect and *when*, the astrologer can make predictions and forecasts for you.

Nothing is written in stone; you can change anything. Think of your birth chart this way—you were given a "special plan" for your life the day you were born. There are certain things you want to accomplish, to overcome or to do in your lifetime. There are talents you need to develop, lessons you want to learn and people you want to love. Your chart holds all of these opportunities and more. The key to achieving your potential, is knowing what assets

it holds and taking action to reach that potential. Timing is everything. Your chart can reveal the best times to go after your dreams,
when you'll have the most luck and even when the energies of the
cosmos are challenging you.

Let's say three people named Jim, Janice and Joe have the
exact same chart. That doesn't happen often, but let's just say it
did. All three charts showed they were born with beautiful voices.
All revealed they would be very successful in a career using their
voice. Jim's parents recognized their son had musical ability. So, at
an early age they enrolled him in singing classes, drama and
dance. He practiced for years refining his voice. He went on Broad-
way auditions and couldn't get a break. But he kept going. He kept
pushing. In his late 20s, he landed a record deal and is now a
multi-million dollar recording artist. His parents had a chart done
when he was born, understood his potential, helped Jim on his
path and acted when the "timing" was right. You've heard people
say "I was at the right place at the right time". Astrology can give
you those "times". The potential was there, in Jim's chart, but *he*
had to make things happen. He's using his voice to make music
and has now become very famous and very rich by doing so.

Janice has the same chart. Everyone compliments her on her
pretty voice. She sang in school musicals but decided computers
were a sure bet to make money. So she got a degree in computer
science and teaching. She's a sales manager and trainer in the
computer industry making a decent income. She's using her voice
to sell and to teach others. Untapped potential? Perhaps. It's all in
the way you perceive it.

Then there's Joe, who sings in the shower. He didn't know
anything about his chart until he got a reading at a psychic party
when he was 18. The astrologer told him he had a beautiful voice
and should use it to make money. He didn't take the advice seriously. Over the next few years, Joe got married, worked in a con-

struction business and had a couple of kids. Everyone tells him he should sing in a band or get into the radio business. He's still singing in the shower.

Are you Joe? Do you have untapped talent? Is there potential you don't even know about? You may find it in your astrology chart. It can tell you what you are "here" to do—what your soul purpose and path are. It can give you the best times to act on opportunities and the periods to just "hold back" and wait. Perhaps your chart shows fame and fortune in your fifties rather than your early twenties. It may show you're not going to live an extravagant lifestyle, but a far simpler one. Your life lesson could be that of raising a family, rather than running a corporation. We're all here for different reasons. Whatever your life lesson is, it will be right there . . . in your birth chart!

Timing is everything and that's the nice thing about astrology, it gives you a time frame to work with. But don't look just at the "big picture". There are growth and potential in each and every day of our lives. Some days are bigger and brighter than others are. And then there are those days when nothing goes right. We may need to review and adjust the path we're on. We need the challenging periods just as much as the fortunate ones. I have a picture my daughter drew years ago that says "There can't be rainbows without rain". It sits on my desk to remind me to accept and be thankful for the cloudy times too.

Just as clouds can bring rain and rain can bring rainbows, the planets are believed to bring certain influences at specific times. The planets in our solar system are in constant motion and make positive and challenging aspects when they *conjunct, oppose* or *square* other planets. A professional astrologer can interpret your chart and tell you *what* to expect and *when*, in any area of your life. Use astrology as a tool. Take the information and see how it works for you.

Astrology can also give us insight to the many cycles of our lives. Some are very specific time frames for luck and advancement. There are also life cycles that generally cause challenges and change. Let's look at them from the toddler years all the way up to the late eighties.

We all experience the same life cycles around the same age, but our issues and lessons may be different depending on what we need to learn in our lifetime.

Here's a list of the Planets we'll be dealing with in this chapter

Sun—Vitality, who you are

Moon—Our emotional side

Jupiter—Good luck, benefit, abundance

Saturn—The great teacher, challenging, difficult and unyielding (If you pass the tests Saturn brings, you'll be rewarded.)

Pluto—Death and regeneration, power struggles, ultimate change, control

Mars—Energy, anger, action

Mercury—Communication

Uranus—Quick and sudden changes

Neptune—Illusion, psychic ability, deception and the unforeseen

How planets aspect one another

Conjunction—Either very positive or extremely challenging, depending on the individual planets

Trine—Good for opportunity

Opposition—Struggles, hardships, sometimes opportunity because of other people

Square—Challenging aspects

Now let's take a look at our

Life Cycles

Age 2½ years—We call this period the Terrible Twos. This is the cycle when the sweet little baby suddenly becomes a holy terror! The child acts up, claims his own identity and wants to take charge! He has a tremendous amount of energy and doesn't miss a lick!

Astrological Influence—This is the first Mars Return. Mars, the action, war-like planet, comes back to where it was positioned in the child's chart at birth, causing all types of independent stands. Kids are ready to take risks and chances. There is a Mars Return every 2.5 years but parents notice it more the first time it rolls around.

Age 3—Children are as bold as they can be. They want to do everything the big kids do. Some kids get a little arrogant and feel that the world centers completely around them.

Astrological Influence—Jupiter Square Jupiter. Kids feel more enthusiasm for life. They feel confident to take chances.

Age 7½—Around this age, kids become very cocky. They think they know it all. The little angel who was thrilled to see her parents after school, is now arguing about her clothes, the food she eats and bedtime hour. Boundaries are set and the child feels that everyone is restricting her.

Astrological Influence—The first Saturn Square Saturn. Saturn, the planet of restrictions, delays and tests, makes the child feel overwhelmed at times. They must take responsibility now for their actions. This cycle corresponds with the age of reason.

AGE 9½—Important people will come into the child's life. They will touch their lives and have a major impact in some way. Children may meet a mentor or special teacher. Some may be obsessed with a music star or actor. Family additions bring new siblings that will alter life as they know it. Usually during this transit, a new person enters and has a special purpose for being in the youngster's life. Sometimes, relationships end, as in the passing of a grandparent. Relationships and/or personal issues now have a life-long lasting effect.

Astrological Influence—Node Opposition and the 9 year Saturn Square. Nodes are said to be karmic or to bring a "fated" quality to a person's life. There are great lessons to be learned now.

Age 12—Children start to expand their world. They experience physical growth spurts. Boys begin puberty and girls may experience their first menstruation. Opportunities come knocking. They may be recognized for some sort of school or sport achievement. Things tend to go well. This is also a time that kids are given a little more freedom. Parents are apt to leave them home alone now. Many start getting an allowance or baby sitting and lawn cutting jobs.

Astrological Influence—The Jupiter Return. The lucky planet Jupiter bestows many blessings on the child. This is a time of great expansion and opportunity. It comes around every 12 years.

Age 14—Young teens are now viewing their world as something larger than their family, their school and circle of friends. Kids around age 14 wonder how they fit into society and what their role should be. They are excited about life and all that it has to offer. Friendships are very important. Kids start to stand up to their parents and question everything. They are eager to strike out and create their own identity.

Astrological Influence—Uranus Sextile Uranus and First Saturn Opposition. During the first Saturn Opposition, kids learn that they have to buckle down to succeed or be accepted into a good college one day. There are more social and after-school activity demands in addition to homework. This often coincides with the freshman year in high school.

Age 21—The first real job comes along. This is also a time of tests and challenges. Young adults may have problems with authority figures and bosses at work. They could go through several jobs over the course of the next year or two. There is a desire to break free, but the limitations of money, long work hours and college studies, hold one back. Tensions build easily. On the up side, people get married now, graduate from college and think they're home free. Different types of responsibilities set in. However, they are finally able to pursue and create the type of life they desire.

Astrological Influence—The first Uranus Square brings unexpected problems and disappointments, because of other people and relationships.

Age 24—A year-long period of growth and good luck. Young adults want to settle down and get married. They are thinking about how many kids they will have. They graduate from college and are working up the career ladder. Some are moving permanently away from their family and childhood home. There are opportunities to travel and meet all sorts of new people.

Astrological Influence—Second Jupiter Return. The lucky planet comes back again after a 12-year hiatus and drops opportunity in the young adult's lap. The transit lasts for 12 months.

Around Age 27—The person may feel depressed. It's not because of the heavier, more publicized "Saturn Return" either. There's another transit at work here. One feels older and as if life is passing them by. They feel a need to "make things happen". If they're not married, they feel lonely. If they're married, they feel trapped.

Astrological Influence—The Lunar (moon) Return. The moon rules our emotional state. Therefore, much that comes out of this transit has to do with our feelings. Think logically now if you can!

Around Age 29?—People are forced by the universe to grow up! This is a major cycle. You will break down to rebuild life on a more solid basis. Anything that is not working for you, you'll get rid of. That includes bad marriages, dead-end jobs and stale environments. These folks also put down roots. New careers blossom, major moves and lifestyle changes occur. Some singles get married. Many people have children now.

Astrological Influence—First Saturn Return. This cycle comes around only every 29.5 years, and it's a *big* one. Any decisions you make and lessons you failed to learn will have an effect about 30 years from now, during the Second Saturn Return. At that point, you'll have to deal with the consequences. This cycle lasts for 2.5 years. You'll remember these years well!

Age 36—This is a positive time for career prospects. The person feels like they've "made it". Watch out for your metabolism slowing down. It's time for the middle-age spread. Women, if married with children, stop worrying about their biological clock. Things go rather well.

Astrological Influence—The Jupiter Return. We last saw this aspect at age 24. It won't come around now for another 12 years.

Age 36 to 38—*Watch out,* this transit is a big one! It's one of the most important transits in your life. Why? If you're married, this is the cycle in which the union could fall apart. By this time, you and your spouse have probably amassed some small fortune. You may own a home, have several cars, a growing 401K plan and a pension. If there is a divorce, you could lose it all. This is also a period in which you may get in a financial bind. Most people around this age want more materials things out of life. It's time to finance the dream home, buy a boat and take the European vacation. They think they deserve it. They'll live beyond their means; get home equity loans, max out credit cards and spend, spend, spend! This is also an age in which women are considering plastic surgery and men are signing up for gym memberships.

Astrological Influence—Saturn Square Saturn, following the Saturn Return. You've just gotten over the challenges of the Saturn Return 5 or so years ago, then the Saturn Square hits again. There are still more lessons to learn.

I look at the first 40 years of life as a time for growth, learning who we are and establishing ourselves in the world. The next stage of our life begins around age 40. I believe each decade brings with it a new lesson and a theme.

THE 40s

*We reflect on what we've accomplished
in our life. We still see ourselves as young.
There is still time to accomplish things we desire.*

THE 50s

*We begin reviewing our life like never
before. We're not old, but we're not young.
Some people panic. Others relax.*

THE 60s

*The theme is acceptance. We accept who
we are and don't care what others think.
We accept the things we cannot change.*

THE 70s

We begin sharing our true wisdom with others.
We feel compelled to teach or to give back to society.
We tell the younger generation about life and the lessons
we've learned. We may teach grandchildren
how to cook, read or about our family's history.

THE 80s

We should be celebrated. This is a time of
thanks for all we've done for others. It is also
a karmic time, when we reap what we've sowed.

Now let's go onto the second part of our life cycles, also the period in which many people are believed to experience the mid-life crisis.

Mid 40s—The mid-life crisis can start about age 42 and linger for 2 or more years. This is the time when balding men grow what hair they have left and take Viagra®. They buy red sports cars and date younger women. The women who experience this transit feel the empty nest syndrome or yearn for a more exciting life. Both sexes could enter into affairs if the influences are right. At some point, they're not sure what they want out of life. They don't feel young anymore. They want to grab the brass ring one more time . . . before it's too late.

Astrological Influence—Uranus Opposite Uranus coincides with the Saturn Square Saturn aspect. Uranus is a planet of change and Saturn a planet of restriction. You may feel as if changes are forced upon you, against your will. You feel restricted because of a situation or someone and want to break free.

Ages 42 to 46—People get dumped or fired. If you're in a dead end relationship or even a long-term marriage, your partner could suddenly leave. At work, younger, bright-eyed co-workers appear. Management knows they'll work for less and be eager to please. Relationships of all sorts could prove troublesome.

Astrological Influence—Saturn Opposite Saturn. On an opposition, problems arise beyond your control because of other people. You may feel as if you have no control over a situation and are being pushed in a new direction, whether you like it or not. Karmically, these circumstances were meant to happen, and good will be the result.

Around Age 48—Menopause may start to set in for women. Some people may consider a buy-out or early retirement package at work. Others will have great opportunities for career advancements. Mortgages will be burned. There is more of a carefree attitude about life. Kids move out of the house. There's happiness and good times!

Astrological Influence—Fourth Jupiter Return. That lucky planet takes its turn to meet up with you again. It's a welcome influence compared to the past several years.

Age 50—People start thinking about their future. Will there be enough money for retirement? Can I get all of the bills paid off? Should I retire early? Can I really afford to send Junior to college now? These are all worries that may come up around the age 50 mark. You'll start seriously considering your future as never be-

fore. If you've planned well, you will feel secure. If not, you're going to be concerned about finances over the next year or so.

Astrological Influence—Saturn Square Saturn. The Saturn Square brings pressure to do something, or at least to recognize it. There are challenges now and many of them are trying.

Age 54 to 55—This is a time of spiritual reflection. You come to terms with who you are and where you've been. You are more optimistic about the future and are looking at life in a deeper, more meaningful way. You are completely honest with yourself. Generally, you'll feel good about who you are and what you stand for.

Astrological Influence—Neptune Trine Neptune. You will feel less self-centered as Neptune gives you more empathy for others. Psychic abilities are also increasing.

Age 58 to 60—There's a lot happening in this period. This is considered a major cycle; one of the most interesting in over 30 years of your life. Many changes are in store. Whatever it was you were supposed to learn during your First Saturn Return around age 29, you'll have done so or there will be harsh lessons now.

However, this can also be a time of great reward. Your accomplishments are noticed. You've come to the point in life where you're doing away with the things you don't need. Some people retire, move and get a divorce. Others get married for the second time. There are those who must also deal with elderly parent issues. And grown-up children could be moving back into your home during their own crisis. You thought you'd have time for yourself, but the outside world is making many demands on your time, money and energy. Old structures break down. The areas of life, you thought were stable and reliable may change drastically.

Astrological Influence—Pluto Square Pluto, the Second Saturn Return. Squares usually bring in obstacles because of others and Pluto rules death and regeneration. So you will be forced by others or the universe to make life-altering decisions. Saturn is back once again to teach you great lessons and to set the stage for another 30 years.

Age 60—Things appear to be easing up a bit. People feel as if they have new opportunities and are more optimistic about life. They can see a "light at the end of the tunnel". Retirement and social security begin in a few years. The kids are out of the house (hopefully) and there are exciting plans for the future.

Astrological Influence—Fifth Jupiter Return. Coming back after a 12-year hiatus, Jupiter brings blessings and opportunities to those who are willing to take risks and are open to receive.

Age 63—People are looking at retiring now or within the next 2 years. They are making plans to adjust to a new lifestyle. Major changes occur. Some people could be taking care of elderly parents or relatives. Others are enjoying their second childhood by treating the grandchildren. Some are selling off the family farm and downsizing to live a more carefree life. Many people find they don't know what do with themselves as they approach a more leisurely period.

Astrological Influence—Uranus Square Uranus. This transit occurs only twice in your life, once in your early twenties and again in the early sixties. It signifies major changes that force you to alter your path and plans for the future.

Age 71—At this age you recognize the strength of the foundations you've built, along with the consequences of the decisions you've made over the past 50 years. For example, if you were a heavy smoker, you may have breathing problems now. If you were careful with money and saved, you will be financially comfortable. However, old issues that you didn't address in years past may arise and be more difficult to handle now.

Astrological Influence—Saturn Opposite Saturn. There are likely to be health and money issues now. Your spouse may be ill. You'll reminisce a lot, remembering old war stories and past family history.

Age 78—You have real concerns now with the aging process. You'll feel older and have to take care of health ailments. This is also a time of low energy. People start taking afternoon naps.

Astrological Influence—Saturn Square Saturn is a time when your energy is depleted. Some areas of your life will go through tests and challenges. You may even experience an identity crisis.

Age 82—People get more religious. That's why you find mostly older folks in church. Sometimes, people start to act a little goofy. They don't care what others think of them. Your kids or other family members may think you're losing your mind. This is a time

when forgetfulness or memory loss sets in. Older folks become more rebellious too as they are afraid of losing their personal freedom. Sometimes a driver's license can be revoked or medical problems keep them from an active lifestyle.

Astrological Influence—Neptune Opposite Neptune and Uranus Opposite Uranus. The Neptune aspect makes one become more fanatic about something or lose reality. Sometime people become paranoid. The Uranus aspects mean the person is resisting change brought on by society or other people. For example, an older person hollers at their children, "I am not going into a nursing home!"

Age 84—At this point in your life, you will start to enjoy the simple pleasures it has to offer. You will not fret about bills and taxes. They'll be paid. You won't allow yourself to worry about mundane things, but will appreciate your family, your home and those you hold dear. You are very wise now and coming into a new evolutionary period.

Astrological Influence—The Uranus Return. This transit sometimes occurs right after you were born and then not again until age 84. It signifies that life as you knew it is ending and that there will be positive changes ahead.

Age 85—At this time in our life there are major changes occurring that are beyond our control. These are considered lifestyle changes. It's as if our world is being broken down and rebuilt. Nothing stays the same. Some people lose their spouse or get sick.

Others sell everything and move away. Many people feel isolated during this period and just want to dwell on the past. Others are taking care of an ill spouse. It is a period much like you experienced at age 29 and between ages 58 and 60.

Astrological influence—The Third Saturn Return—A major cycle of your life is closing. Great new changes are about to take place, but you must let the past go. The year before the Saturn Return, many changes have already taken place within you. It is best to roll with the punches now and life will be better for it. This could be one of the most spiritual times of your life.

TWO

Lucky Jupiter

★ ★ ★ You learned a little bit about astrology in the first chapter. This chapter is dedicated to two very important transits of two very important planets; Jupiter and Saturn.

Jupiter gets all the credit but Saturn does all the work. Jupiter is considered by many to be a lucky and beneficial planet, while Saturn is considered restrictive, challenging and thought to bring crisis, hardship and tests. There's some truth to both of these statements. However, there's much more to consider. Saturn can be a great teacher. It is powerful. Jupiter can bring too much of a good thing and therefore be problematic. We're going to take a look at both and tell you when these two life-altering planets will have a major impact on you.

Jupiter takes 12 years to pass through each sign of the zodiac.

It lasts approximately 12 months in every sign. Jupiter usually brings great opportunities, good health, vitality, financial blessings and many other wonderful things. It's important to know exactly when Jupiter will conjunct your sun sign, so you can prepare and plan ahead to "push the envelope". Remember, we discussed earlier that your birth chart is divided into 12 "houses" and each represents a part of life? Jupiter will spend 1 year in every house as it transits around your chart.

Think of Jupiter as taking a trip. He will spend approximately 12 months in the first house and then proceed to the second house, and so on. The first house in your chart represents you, your physical self and personal interests. When Jupiter comes to visit that area of the natal chart, it will expand your interests. It will also expand your waistline! Jupiter visits correspond with things expanding or an abundance of something. So expect good health, great opportunities and personal and physical growth.

I mentioned earlier that Jupiter can be too much of a good thing sometimes. You could put on weight on easily when it conjuncts your first house. You can overspend when it moves through the second. You may become a workaholic when it reaches the 10 house, career.

The following several pages will tell you how Jupiter affects each house in your chart. I've shown which sign Jupiter is in for during all periods for the next 12 years. You'll want to take note when Jupiter comes to visit and be prepared to receive its many gifts.

Jupiter Transits

Here's the guide for the next 12 years for each sign. First find the period in which you're interested. Next find your sign in the list for that period—beside it is the house that Jupiter is in that year. Then go to the "Jupiter Through the Houses" section and read about Jupiter in that house.

For example, say you're a Virgo. To find out about how Jupiter's transits will affect you during the late summer of 2002, you see that this time period is under the heading "Jupiter in Leo". Looking down the listing, you see that Jupiter is in Virgo's twelfth house. So you then turn to the "Jupiter Through the Houses" section, next, and page through until you find the description for the twelfth house.

Note. If you know your ascendant (rising sign), for more accuracy, read about that too. If you don't know it, a professional astrologer can give you this information but you must supply your birth date, time of birth and place of birth.

JUPITER IN LEO
Aug. 2, 2002–Aug. 27, 2003

Aries—5th house
Taurus—4th
Gemini—3rd
Cancer—2nd
Leo—1st
Virgo—12th
Libra—11th
Scorpio—10th
Sagittarius—9th
Capricorn—8th
Aquarius—7th
Pisces—6th

JUPITER IN VIRGO
Aug. 28, 2003–Sept. 25, 2004

Aries—6th House
Taurus—5th
Gemini—4th
Cancer—3rd
Leo—2nd
Virgo—1st
Libra—12th
Scorpio—11th
Sagittarius—10th
Capricorn—9th
Aquarius—8th
Pisces—7th

JUPITER IN LIBRA
Sept. 26, 2004–Oct. 26, 2005

Aries—7th
Taurus—6th
Gemini—5th
Cancer—4th
Leo—3rd
Virgo—2nd
Libra—1st
Scorpio—12th
Sagittarius—11th
Capricorn—10th
Aquarius—9th
Pisces—8th

JUPITER IN SCORPIO
Oct. 27, 2005–Nov. 24, 2006

Aries—8th house
Taurus—7th
Gemini—6th
Cancer—5th
Leo—4th
Virgo—3rd
Libra—2nd
Scorpio—1st
Sagittarius—12th
Capricorn—11th
Aquarius—10th
Pisces—9th

JUPITER IN SAGITTARIUS
Nov. 25, 2006–Dec. 18, 2007

Aries—9th house
Taurus—8th
Gemini—7th
Cancer—6th
Leo—5th
Virgo—4th
Libra—3rd
Scorpio—2nd
Sagittarius—1st
Capricorn—12th
Aquarius—11th
Pisces—10th

JUPITER IN CAPRICORN
Dec. 19, 2007–Jan. 4, 2009

Aries—10th house
Taurus—9th
Gemini—8th
Cancer—7th
Leo—6th
Virgo—5th
Libra—4th
Scorpio—3rd
Sagittarius—2nd
Capricorn—1st
Aquarius—12th
Pisces—11th

JUPITER IN AQUARIUS

Jan. 5, 2009–Jan. 18, 2010

Aries—11th house
Taurus—10th
Gemini—9th
Cancer—8th
Leo—7th
Virgo—6th
Libra—5th
Scorpio—4th
Sagittarius—3rd
Capricorn—2nd
Aquarius—1st
Pisces—12th

JUPITER IN PISCES

Jan. 19, 2010–Jun 6, 2010
Sept. 10, 2010–Jan. 22, 2011

Aries—2nd house
Taurus—12th
Gemini—11th
Cancer—9th
Leo—8th
Virgo—7th
Libra—6th
Scorpio—5th
Sagittarius—4th
Capricorn—3rd
Aquarius—2nd
Pisces—1st

JUPITER IN ARIES

Jun 7, 2010–Sept. 9, 2010
Jan. 23, 2011–Jun. 4, 2011

Aries—1st house
Taurus—12th
Gemini—11th
Cancer—10th
Leo—9th
Virgo—8th
Libra—7th
Scorpio—6th
Sagittarius—5th
Capricorn—4th
Aquarius—3rd
Pisces—2nd

JUPITER IN TAURUS

Jun. 5, 2011–Jun. 11, 2012

Aries—2nd house
Taurus—1st
Gemini—12th
Cancer—11th
Leo—10th
Virgo—9th
Libra—8th
Scorpio—7th
Sagittarius—6th
Capricorn—5th
Aquarius—4th
Pisces—3rd

JUPITER IN GEMINI
Jun. 12, 2012–Jun. 26, 2013

Aries—3rd house
Taurus—2nd
Gemini—1st
Cancer—12th
Leo—11th
Virgo—10th
Libra—9th
Scorpio—8th
Sagittarius—7th
Capricorn—6th
Aquarius—5th
Pisces—4th

JUPITER IN CANCER
Jun. 27, 2013–Jul. 16, 2014

Aries—4th house
Taurus—3rd
Gemini—2nd
Cancer—1st
Leo—12th
Virgo—11th
Libra—10th
Scorpio—9th
Sagittarius—8th
Capricorn—7th
Aquarius—6th
Pisces—5th

JUPITER IN LEO
Jul. 17, 2014–Aug. 11, 2015

Aries—5th house
Taurus—4th
Gemini—3rd
Cancer—2nd
Leo—1st
Virgo—12th
Libra—11th
Scorpio—10th
Sagittarius—9th
Capricorn—8th
Aquarius—7th

Jupiter Through the Houses

FIRST HOUSE

There will be many opportunities and a major expansion of your interests and desires. You will feel good, but watch out for weight gain. You may put an extra 10 pounds on without even trying! You may find that your metabolism is slowing down. Many wonderful things can happen now. If there is something you have your heart set on, go after it. This could be one of the most fortunate times in over a decade. It's the big "pay-off year!" Be ready for it.

Things You Should Do

1. Expand your interests.
2. Focus on You!
3. Watch your weight.
4. Improve your physical appearance.
5. Take risks and chances.

SECOND HOUSE

You could spend a lot of money—but could make a million too. Financial opportunities drop right into your lap. This is the year one may get a raise, inheritance or be just plain lucky. There's also a tendency to overspend and accumulate a lot of things you really don't need. You could be very extravagant this year.

Things You Should Do

1. Ask for a raise.
2. Invest money.
3. Look at every financial opportunity that comes your way.
4. Don't overspend.
5. Apply for a loan, scholarship or grant.

THIRD HOUSE

You should be able to take some great trips and dream vacations. It's a super time for communication, contracts and negotiations. Many people buy new cars and other vehicles. There will be more time spent with neighbors; you'll just enjoy visiting. Relationships with in-laws could improve. Sibling relationships are favored as well. It's a very creative year.

Things You Should Do

1. Take your dream trip.
2. Buy a new car.
3. Make peace with your siblings.
4. Get to know your neighbors.
5. Negotiate and communicate.
6. Write a book.
7. Buy a computer.

FOURTH HOUSE

Home and family issues take center stage. Many people expand their real estate holdings. They may buy or sell property, add on to their current dwelling or remodel. There may be expansion in the family. People get married and put down roots. In general, there's a sense of pride and peace in the family structure. On a spiritual level, the fourth house represents the soul and this year your soul grows in marvelous ways.

Things You Should Do

1. Move, buy, sell real estate.
2. Mend fences in the family.
3. Have a baby.

4. Get in touch with you inner self.

5. Have a family reunion.

FIFTH HOUSE

Expansion in the area of love affairs is expected. It's a great time to meet someone new and exciting. This is also a period in which your relationship runs smoothly. Kids are a joy. Jupiter in the fifth house can create a pregnancy too. Lucky times are here. Fly to Atlantic City or Las Vegas now. Gambling is favored. You'll feel more like playing. Hobbies, sports and creative endeavors could take up a lot of your free time.

Some Things You Should Do

1. Gamble.

2. Expand your hobbies.

3. Play sports.

4. Look for a new romance.

5. Get pregnant.

6. Be creative.

7. Spend time with your children.

SIXTH HOUSE

Watch out for weight gain! You could pack some pounds on now. Your sixth house rules health, too, so you should be feeling good. If any health concerns do arise, know that you will be protected and have a great chance of improving and overcoming any problems. Jupiter in the sixth is also good for getting a new pet. It's a time for your work to expand, especially if you are involved in a field that is service oriented. You may find yourself becoming more involved in community volunteer work and fund-raisers. The sixth house represents old love affairs, so don't be surprised if the ex-boyfriend or girlfriend shows up at your doorstep.

Some Things You Should Do

1. Watch for weight gain.
2. Get involved in health and fitness routines.
3. Look for new work opportunities.
4. Pay attention to details.
5. Clean the garage and organize your life.
6. Enjoy relationships with co-workers.

SEVENTH HOUSE

These are positive marriage and commitment years. You could walk down the aisle or at least meet a very special person who may lead to a deeper commitment. When Jupiter passes through the seventh house, love and relationships are the focus. If you're flying solo, you'll meet someone wonderful. If already attached, your relationship grows deeper and runs smoother. Partnerships of all kinds are favored from business to love and family. Legal issues that arise will be settled in one's favor. Help comes from other people. This is not a year to look a gift horse in the mouth; accept kindness. Most people you meet will be positive and a benefit to you.

Some Things You Should Do

1. Get married.
2. Develop new relationships.
3. Enter into business partnerships.
4. Proceed with legal affairs.

EIGHTH HOUSE

Jupiter through the eighth highlights more money, sex and spirituality. The eighth house rules other people's money and resources so expect benefits now. Your mate could get a raise. You may receive an inheritance. There's a better benefit package at work. Money comes through surprise sources. You run into good deals and sales. This is a time to pay off debt, refinance or apply for a loan. Lots of credit card applications come in the mail. On a spiritual level, your psychic abilities are growing. It's a wonderful time to study the occult.

Some Things You Should Do

1. Pay off debt.
2. Apply for loans and grants.
3. Get scholarships.
4. Find great deals and bargains.
5. Have good sex and lots of it.

NINTH HOUSE

The Ninth House rules long distance travel, education, legal matters, publishing and recognition. When Jupiter moves into your ninth house, it is a very important time. You get more recognition at work. You replace what you "think" of yourself with true knowledge. It's no longer, "I'm pretty good at my job". It's, "I know I am good and I deserve a promotion!" You are more self-assured. Those in high-ranking positions notice you. This is also a great time for long distance and overseas travel. Most people go somewhere, usually when they least expect it! Legal matters fare well. Writers should be receiving royalty checks and pushing their work now. Religion becomes very important in a person's life or one experiences spiritual growth. Going to school to earn a degree is favored as well. This is also the house of in-laws and older relatives such as grandparents, aunts and uncles. They could be a source of happiness at this time.

Some Things To Do

1. Travel to Europe.
2. Publish a book.
3. Take a class.
5. Sue someone.
6. Spend time with the in-laws.
7. Get your tarot cards read.
8. Go to church.
9. Finish your degree.
10. Toot your horn at work.

TENTH HOUSE

When Jupiter hits your midheaven or tenth house, all that you have worked hard for, pays off. You will be lucky. Things fall in your lap, mainly career offers. You will be in the spotlight whether you like it or not. There's much recognition, praise, promotion and opportunity. Some people get married when Jupiter hits their tenth house.

Some Things You Should Do

1. Ask for a promotion.
2. Start your own business.
3. Expect reward and recognition.
4. Get married.

ELEVENTH HOUSE

By the time Jupiter accesses the eleventh house, it's time to talk cold, hard cash. You made your way to the top with Jupiter in the tenth, now the money comes when Jupiter reaches the eleventh. This is also the house of hopes, dreams and wishes. You could see many of your fondest dreams come true. You'll be more involved with social circles. Friendships are very important. You'll probably meet new and interesting people. It could be a fun-filled year.

Some Things You Should Do

1. Make new friends.
2. Get involved in the political or social scene.
3. Ask for a raise at work.
4. See your dreams come true.

TWELFTH HOUSE

Most twelfth house transits prove to be troublesome, but this one can actually be quite rewarding; though you may not notice the benefits as you do with other house transits. During this period, a special person or spiritual advisor may enter your life. They may come in the form of a new friend or acquaintance. This guru need not be a famous person—just an ordinary guy. There are also subconscious energies at work. Anything that has been bothering you on a deep level can be healed. This is a wonderful time to let go of past hurts and pain. Many people gain true spiritual wisdom and knowledge. Others feel they can release past pain and move forward. Still, many grow to new and deeper spiritual depths.

Some Things You Should Do

1. Welcome people from your past.
2. Expect good karmic returns.
3. Heal old emotional wounds.
4. Expand psychic abilities.
5. Feel at peace with yourself.
6. Let go of things that are holding you back.

THREE

$\mathcal{C}$he $\mathcal{P}$lanet $\mathcal{S}$aturn

Because of the effect it has on us, I believe Saturn is one of the most important planets in our solar system. It represents structure and discipline, lesson and tests, reward and punishment. As Saturn transits your natal chart, it brings tension and challenge to the house it hits.

Most people who know very little about astrology say Saturn is a bad planet. It really isn't. There are a great many rewards, but only after you deal with the lesson that Saturn is trying to teach you. Saturn takes about 2? years to go through each sign, so you should pay close attention to the house or area of your life that it's transiting.

Many times there will be losses. Generally, these are losses that are needed. For example, when Saturn transits your tenth house of career and work, you may get fired or your company will close. But, all along, you may have hated your job. Perhaps, you could no longer grow as a soul. Maybe the company held you back from realizing your highest potential. You stayed on anyway, because you needed the money and didn't know what else to do. So Saturn came along and really shook things up. It forced you to experience extreme tension and problems on the job so you'd consider other options. Or it simply took away what wasn't working.

At other times, Saturn in the tenth can bring great reward. Maybe you've worked hard for years and never gotten the recognition due to you. If you've laid a solid foundation, Saturn will reward you for these efforts, say with a promotion, raise or new position. That's the way Saturn works; it's a teacher. Think of Saturn this way; it will bring you tests and challenges. It will make you work hard. If you deal with each challenge or crisis as it comes up—rather than ignoring the lessons—you'll be rewarded, perhaps in even bigger ways than the planet Jupiter rewards you.

Some people experience depression, sadness, or physical or emotional losses during a Saturn transit. Some Saturn transits are easier than others. But if you go with the flow, be open to what the universe is bringing you and don't resist, Saturn's pressure for change will mean you'll grow spiritually and life will be better because of this transit.

In 1994, I counseled a woman who was going through such a transit. Saturn was on her sun sign in Pisces. Now, many of you have heard me say that Pisces is not the easiest sign to be. These folks are always going through a crisis. I was worried about this lady because Saturn was ready to make a major aspect in her chart. I counseled her about impending challenges and how to look at Saturn in a positive way. I took extra time with her to make sure she understood what this transit meant and how best to deal with it.

Apparently, she took my advice. About 2 years later, I saw her again and she said these were the most wonderful years of her life. She looked at how Saturn was "helping" her work to a higher spiritual level. Yes, she confirmed there had been many losses. She got a divorce, lost her job and one of her parents died. Many nuisances occurred but she looked at these endings as things that were supposed to happen and accepted them. She was forced to try new things, and thus had enjoyed many new experiences. She was actually thrilled with the way her life was turning out, all because she handled her Saturn transit from a spiritual perspective. She choose not to hang on to things she was supposed to release. Therefore, this woman was able to accept the new opportunities and rewards Saturn was bringing her.

Saturn never takes away anything you truly need, only things that outlive their usefulness and, yes, that means relationships too. We all procrastinate. We hang on to dead-end relationships and limited incomes. We refuse to move ahead. Either we're scared, lazy or just plain too content. So Saturn shakes things up for us and creates a better life . . . eventually. You will change dramatically inside and out after a Saturn transit. You will be a different person. More than likely, new and improved. You'll know you can make it through anything!

The good news is that Saturn comes around only every 30 years to visit each sign. But when it does, it really cleans house! I say prepare yourself ahead of time, before Saturn hits. For example, if Saturn will be transiting your second house of money next year, pay all of your debts off now. Don't take on any large payments and prepare to scale back. You'll be living within your means. Put money aside for the next 2? years, because you will probably need it.

A few years back, I recognized a tough financial period was ahead. Saturn was going into one of my money houses in my chart and I was going to be ready for it! I put extra cash away. I'm glad I did, because when Saturn hit and work slowed down, I didn't have the pressure of dealing with less income. I knew even in lean times, I would be able to meet my basic bills. It took a lot of pressure off of me.

When Saturn was in my seventh house of marriage, I realized this was the year I could get a divorce. I knew it was coming, and yes, my husband and I did have our share of problems. But understanding why and how long the problems were going to last, helped me a great deal. I didn't argue with him, I let him get away with a lot! I made sure things didn't get out of hand, and I wrote an uplifting affirmation to myself that I carried around in my purse for almost 3 years.

The "Saturn" letter helped me immensely. Whenever I got depressed or angry, I could always blame it on Saturn, and I'd pull out my letter. It made me feel calm and more at ease. Therefore I didn't react in an erratic way about what was going on in my marriage. I sat back and analyzed what I was learning: patience, compromise and understanding. I let Saturn show me the way. I learned a lot.

When Saturn lifted, 2½ long years later, it seemed as if all of our problems had vanished. We were truly content and never fought. Nothing dramatic happened. Rather, there was a feeling of security and contentment in our marriage. I feel as if we can weather any storm now.

I think the hardest transit of Saturn is when it conjuncts a person's sun sign. Everything in their life is tested; their job, love life, health money, family, and attitude. It seems as if there's one problem after another. But like everyone else, you can get through it too. Those Pisces, Aries, Taurus and Gemini people, who went through heavy Saturn transits in the 90's and the early part of the new century, know what I'm talking about.

They're still here, better than ever and stronger because of it. I'm not trying to scare anyone, but if you know ahead of time that you'll be tested and challenged and that certain areas of your life could be turned upside down, wouldn't it be to your advantage to be prepared?

If you really don't want to know what could likely happen, then don't read further. If you're like me and want to be ready, you can learn how to turn a negative into a positive. You can divert problems and stop things from happening. Knowledge is power, and I'd like to give you some power here. There are a few people who never feel affected by transiting Saturn. I wonder if they refuse to deal with reality or are just oblivious to what's going on. Sometimes the effects are not external, but rather, internal. Whatever the case, we all have lessons to learn; otherwise we wouldn't be here.

Saturn and Your Destiny

The Saturn cycle is really about our destiny on this planet. No one has the same destiny as you do, or they would have the exact same horoscope. Many people don't discover their true destiny until they reach their first Saturn Return at age 29? years. It is at this time that one gets in touch with his or her inner being. Before then, you're still conditioned by your upbringing. After that, you take control. It then takes about 7 years for a person to get used to this new "being". The process can culminate around age 35. It's as if you've found a new you! Actually, this period is a time of discovery of who you really are meant to be. There are some people who have more than one destiny.

A DESTINY CAN ONLY BE A DESTINY IF IT HELPS OTHER PEOPLE.

Before you move on to the next lifetime, you must give something back to the universe, something of yourself. Many people's destiny is to teach others. Some people are here to nurture. Others to entertain. There are all kinds of destiny. How do you find yours? All you need to do is ask! You must go within yourself. Meditate. Ask yourself what is it you would like to be doing but think you can't? That's your destiny! And, even if you don't believe you can accomplish it, you must go after it. Your soul will guide you and you have an entire Saturn cycle in which to create it.

The cycle usually corresponds with Saturn transiting your sixth house. (Look in the following pages for the year that Saturn is in your sixth house). You must take the time to talk to your inner self a lot. Usually, there is a new and very special person that appears in your life at this time. They will believe in you. Even if no one else has faith in you, this person will. Pay attention to what he is telling you and only listen to those who believe in you. There is a special soul connection with this mentor. It's usually not a love affair. It has more to do with a person coming in your life as a "guide" or an angel.

You'll also find that, when you go through a Saturn cycle, you are pretty much on your own. You may not get much help from the outside world, because answers to problems don't come from the outside. They come only from within.

Let's take a look at when Saturn will be in your sign and the specific house. If you know your rising sign, read about it too.

SATURN TRANSITS

Find the period you want to look at, then your sign. The house of your chart that Saturn is in during that period appears beside your sign.

SATURN IN GEMINI
2002–Jun. 3, 2003

Aries—3rd house
Taurus—2nd house
Gemini—1st house
Cancer—12th
Leo—11th
Virgo—10th
Libra—9th
Scorpio—8th
Sagittarius—7th
Capricorn—6th
Aquarius—5th
Pisces—4th

SATURN IN CANCER
Jun. 4, 2003–Jul. 16, 2005

Aries—4th house
Taurus—3rd
Gemini—2nd
Cancer—1st
Leo—12th
Virgo—11th
Libra—10th
Scorpio—9th
Sagittarius—8th
Capricorn—7th
Aquarius—6th
Pisces—5th

SATURN IN LEO
Jul. 17, 2005–Sept. 2, 2007

Aries—5th house
Taurus—4th
Gemini—3rd
Cancer—2nd
Leo—1st
Virgo—12th
Libra—11th
Scorpio—10th
Sagittarius—9th
Capricorn—8th
Aquarius—7th
Pisces—6th

SATURN IN VIRGO
Sept. 3, 2007–Oct. 29, 2009

*Retrograde Apr. 8, 2010–
Jul. 21, 2010*

Aries—6th house
Taurus—5th
Gemini—4th
Cancer—3rd
Leo—2nd
Virgo—1st
Libra—12th
Scorpio—11th
Sagittarius—10th
Capricorn—9th
Aquarius—8th
Pisces—7th

SATURN IN LIBRA

Oct. 30, 2009–Apr. 7, 2010
Apr. 8, 2010—Oct. 5, 2012

Aries—7th house
Taurus—6th
Gemini—5th
Cancer—4th
Leo—3rd
Virgo—2nd
Libra—1st
Scorpio—12th
Sagittarius—11th
Capricorn—10th
Aquarius—9th
Pisces—8th

SATURN IN SCORPIO

Oct. 6, 2012–Dec. 23, 2014
Retrograde Jun. 15, 2015–
Sept.17, 2015

Aries—8th house
Taurus—7th
Gemini—6th
Cancer—5th
Leo—4th
Virgo—3rd
Libra—2nd
Scorpio—1st
Sagittarius—12th
Capricorn—11th
Aquarius—10th
Pisces—9th

SATURN IN SAGITTARIUS

Dec. 24, 2014–Jun. 14, 2015
Sept. 18, 2015–Dec. 19, 2017

Aries—9th house
Taurus—8th
Gemini—7th
Cancer—6th
Leo—5th
Virgo—4th
Libra—3rd
Scorpio—2nd
Sagittarius—1st
Capricorn—12th
Aquarius—11th
Pisces—10th

SATURN IN CAPRICORN

Dec. 20, 2017–Mar. 21, 2020

Aries—10th house
Taurus—9th
Gemini—8th
Cancer—7th
Leo—6th
Virgo—5th
Libra—4th
Scorpio—3rd
Sagittarius—2nd
Capricorn—1st
Aquarius—12th
Pisces—11th

Saturn Through the Houses

When Saturn transits the first six houses of your chart (the bottom part), which takes about 15 years, the aspects are very personal. You'll be focusing more on developing abilities and talents, a value system and inner wisdom. You may feel as if you are not gaining much ground. Your focus is on the private part of life and, in essence, you are laying a foundation.

When Saturn moves above the horizon and into the seventh house of your chart, you'll begin to see the gains and rewards of the groundwork you've laid over the past 15 years. If you've laid a good, solid foundation and built a strong base to work from, the rewards will be plentiful. If you goofed off, ignored your path, or lived recklessly, your rewards will be few, if any.

Remember, the first six houses focus on you and your private world. In the seventh through the twelfth, the focus is on the outside world and your interaction with it.

FIRST HOUSE

When Saturn transits the first house, which represents your physical self, you will feel older and take your life much more seriously than ever before. You may also feel restricted or "held back"—as if the pressures of the outside world are pushing against you. You may even look older now. This is also a time for weight loss, so if you need to lose a couple of pounds, they'll come off rather easily. If not, watch out for weight loss related to a health crisis or stress. You'll think about your future and what type of foundations you need to build. You may feel as if people are not as helpful or as kind as before. They are reacting only to the energy of Saturn around you, not to you personally. Try not to be overly sensitive.

Lesson: Learning who you are and how you fit into society.

How To Deal With This: Don't push things. Listen and learn. Recognize that this period is about personal growth and inner as well as external change.

SECOND HOUSE

Saturn transiting the second house forces you to learn major lessons about money and personal resources. You may have to make do with less. Usually the bills will be higher or you'll never seem to have enough money. You will also learn what poverty is. This doesn't mean you'll be broke and homeless, but will feel as if you need to cut back and manage finances wisely. This could be a year of financial crisis. No matter how hard you work, there just isn't enough money to go around. Be careful with your assets. Do not lend money to others at this time or get involved in get-rich schemes. I suggest that, before this transit hits your chart, you "put away" for a rainy day. Live within your means. Your view of material possessions will change drastically over the course of the next 2 years.

Lesson: Learn how to deal with financial issues and understand the difference between material possessions and what really matters in life.

How To Deal With This: Don't overspend. Have a financial plan. Plan for emergencies. Put money away ahead of time.

THIRD HOUSE

Sometimes people get depressed when Saturn moves into their third house. The third house rules communications, mental pursuits and the like. You may feel as if you're cut off from the world, but it may only be in your mind. You're doing a lot of serious thinking. Communication skills are not up to par and therefore more arguments arise. You may feel as if everyone is impatient. It's also a time for car trouble, traffic tickets, fines and travel problems.

If you have siblings, you may worry about their issues or become estranged. Neighbors could be a source of problems too. If you're attending school, expect to work hard and diligently, because there is a tendency to feel overwhelmed by studies. You will be learning a great deal about how much of an impact the spoken word has, and it may change the way you communicate with others. For those of you in communication or creative fields, there could be an onslaught of blockages.

Lessons: How to communicate effectively.

How to Deal with This: Be honest and forthright in all of your communications and dealings.

FOURTH HOUSE

This is the area of home and family, so you will see problems arise within these structures. Some families break apart. There could be divorces or deaths. Usually older parents are a source of concern when Saturn transits the fourth house. It is not a good time to sell a house, because you won't get what you want for it. The sale will be troublesome and slow moving. There will be major repairs and a lot of work that needs to be done around the house.

The fourth house also represents the seat of the soul, so your inner-being is changing. You are finding that you're working from a much deeper level as you examine life's mysteries from a spiritual perspective. Some people move, mostly apprehensively or against their will. Property values decline. It is not a good time to start a major remodeling or addition either. This is a time when most of your attention needs to be centered around the family. Many relatives may have crises or problems. You'll find yourself involved, whether you like it or not. Some people feel like a rubber band, pulled in two directions because of the demands of the family and the job.

Lesson: The dynamics of the family and expanding the soul.

How To Deal With This: Don't take things personally. Go slowly. Don't push or overreact. Try to balance work and family issues. Don't begin a major building or expansion project.

FIFTH HOUSE

Fifth house issues can involve children, creative pursuits, love affairs, hobbies, sports, gambling and investments. If you have children, there may be concerns with problems they are going through. There is a lot of responsibility because of the children. It's not the most favorable time to get pregnant either. If a child is born when Saturn is in one of the parents' fifth house, the child is more of a duty and responsibility than a bundle of joy! Parents may be dealing with their own issues and not able to give the child all of the needed time and attention. Some parents feel overwhelmed or burdened by their youngsters during this period, too. Love affairs can be strained and tested. If you're unattached, a new relationship could come into your life that brings lessons about love and maybe even heartbreak. This is a terrible time to gamble. Don't go to Las Vegas unless you are just visiting the buffets. Also, investments may go down at this time. Stay with tried and true deals, nothing risky. You may not feel creative. Life seems dull.

Lesson: Responsibilities to children, lovers and others.

How To Deal With This: You should avoid getting pregnant now. If you have kids, make sure you have backup childcare plans and take time for yourself periodically. Work with your child's development before this aspect hits. Don't fight with a lover. It takes two to argue! Let go of losing love affairs. The longer you hang on to a bad relationship, the more heartbreak.

SIXTH HOUSE

By the time Saturn reaches the sixth house, you'll be experiencing the last remnants of your personal growth. You will have a better idea of who you are and where you're going in life. This is also a time when your health could be affected. If there are any health issues that pop up now, you should take them seriously and see your doctor. If you're looking to get in shape, work out or lose weight, this is an excellent time. Weight comes off more easily now; for some people, with little effort.

If you have older pets, they may be a source of concern. You will also feel as if all of the nagging details of life are piling up. You'll tire easily of everyday routine but won't be able to escape it. Vacuuming the carpet, taking out the trash, doing dishes and laundry will drive you crazy! You want to break out of the same old routine but can't!

There may be problems with nasty co-workers. You'll find yourself working around a lot of negative people. If you're dissatisfied with your job, you may look elsewhere. There will be stress because of the people at work, not the job itself. So proceed with caution if you want to make changes. This is also a period in which you can get your life in order, tie up any loose ends and get rid of what's not working—for when Saturn moves into the seventh house, you must be ready to meet and greet the world!

Lesson: Discipline at work, service to others and health issues.

How To Deal With This: Work hard and know that it will pay off. Overlook the slights and incompetence of fellow workers. Choose to help them instead. Diet, exercise and watch your health before this transit hits. Takes vitamins and get flu shots.

SEVENTH HOUSE

You are beginning a new 15-year cycle of Saturn transits that push you out into the world. You'll finally start to see rewards for all of your efforts. But Saturn in the seventh house causes you to stop and learn lessons about relationships first. This transit is especially hard on marriages, even the good ones. If you are married or in a long-term committed relationship, obstacles and crisis will arise. The strong marriage will make it through and grow so strong than nothing can break it apart. But the weak ones end. If your marriage or relationship needs to end, let it go. In fact, any relationship that is important to you will go through some type of test. Release the negative ones. The people who are still in your life at the end of this Saturn cycle are supposed to be there. This pertains to family ties and friendships that have faded as well as business partnerships gone sour. The universe is telling you to let go.

However the reverse is true if you're single. This is a time in which you could meet your soul mate and get married. At the same time, you could draw people to you who require a lot of hard work and responsibility. You may draw a new partner who has 10 kids, 5 ex-spouses and tons of debt. You could meet your share of alcoholics, abusive types and people with commitment phobias. So make sure you really get to know someone before falling head-over-heels in love. The fact is, you'll meet many new people and learn to relate to all types of situations.

You are also learning what your true needs are in relationships. What you want from others and what you are willing to give is changing dramatically. You won't be the same person after this transit has passed, when it comes to dealing with others. Try to stay away from legal entanglements, lawsuits and the like, because they could prove to be burdensome. Even though it is likely that someone will make an exit, pass on or that you'll leave a relationship, there is a reason for it. You'll likely understand why, when the transit is over.

Lesson: How to relate to others and the dynamics of relationships, what you need from relationships.

How To Deal With This: Make sure you have excellent legal representation. Work hard if you want to save a good marriage. If you're in a bad or abusive relationship, let it go. Don't hang on. Allow people and partnerships to go without anger, jealousy or remorse. Make sure you put extra energy into your most meaningful relationships now.

EIGHTH HOUSE

Sex, money, death and taxes are all eighth house concerns. Your sex life may be boring or drop off dramatically. You need to keep all receipts, tax, and insurance information. If you've been cheating on your taxes, this could be the year the IRS comes to pay a visit. Your partner's income may decrease, or funds that you depend on may be cut off. It will be harder to get loans and scholarships. Do not lend money or co-sign a loan. Credit card and other debt will seem higher. Do not overextend your credit at this time or it will take years to pay off.

If other aspects in your chart confirm passings, there could be a few funerals to attend. This doesn't always mean someone close to you will die. When Saturn hit my eighth house, a friend from junior high died and there were many acquaintances' funerals to attend, but no major passing in my family.

Work hard now and live within your means. There will be bills beyond your control. Taxes and insurance costs go up. Heating costs and phone bills rise. Keep some cash stashed for a rainy day and double-check all of your financial transactions. Other people could make mistakes that affect you. The positive gain now is that you develop a true purpose in life. You may be setting yourself up for success in the future.

Lesson: To rely on yourself financially, to experience death and rebirth.

How To Deal with This: Put money aside a year before this transit hits. Recognize that death is a part of the life cycle. Study the metaphysical. Don't cheat on your taxes. Check your insurance policies and make sure that all are paid up. Try to get debt under control.

NINTH HOUSE

If you handled the seventh and eighth house transits correctly and learned all of your lessons, progress may be yours. You could be changing your philosophy on life. Your way of thinking and perceiving reality is changing too. Some people switch to a new religion or they grow more spiritual.

Many who are not adequately educated for a career position

may be held back because they lack a certain degree. This is the time to be in school and get the certification and knowledge you need.

Long distance travel is not favorable, especially to foreign countries, as one may have unpleasant experiences. There could be danger or problems associated with foreign people or those of different ethnic backgrounds. You may travel for work, however, and this is a good thing.

Your reputation is on the line and may be challenged by others to see if you really have what it takes to lead and succeed. If you've laid a solid foundation and have been honest and trustworthy in all of your dealings, proper recognition and credit will be yours. However, you may experience problems with authority figures in your profession. There is a sense of being held back by others. It will pass if you work hard and keep an eye on your goals.

Concerns with in-laws, aunts, uncles and the like may arise. Overall, most people feel a need to grow more spiritual. Many get in touch with their higher self and spirit guides at this time.

Lesson: Spiritual growth, preparation for major career expansion.

How To Deal With This: Safeguard your reputation. Work hard and educate yourself as much as possible. Settle out of court if you can, or avoid legal problems altogether. Be ready to accept new challenges and information.

TENTH HOUSE

This is where Saturn really pays off! You will reach a peak now in your career, the outside world and with social status. If you've followed your path and accepted all of the trials and tribulations, if you've learned and grown as a person, you will be greatly rewarded. I have seen some of my country singer clients working in Nashville for years never get a break for years. But when Saturn reached their mid-heaven (tenth house) they signed their first big record deal! If you've been working hard on the job, this is the time for the big promotion. You will be given lots of responsibility. You can handle it. There will be much respect if you deserve it. All you have worked for will be yours! On the other hand, if you failed to build a strong foundation, if you refused to grow and learn, if you misused people along the way, you could crumble and fall.

Here's another scenario: Stuck in a dead-end job? Maybe you can no longer grow in the current position. The universe says you've learned all you can, so the job may be made difficult. You could be fired, laid off and feel trapped in your current surroundings. This is also a time when many people leave and try to find their own path. But if you are on the right path, you will succeed. You should continue to work hard for the next few years . . . very hard, and then you can rest on your laurels for a while. Whether you like the spotlight or not, it will shine brightly upon you.

Lesson: How you fit into society as a whole. Gaining the rewards for a job well done. Realizing that you're on the wrong path and it's time to move in a new direction.

How to Deal with This: Accept the promotions and responsibilities in your career. Work hard. Don't be afraid to make job changes if necessary.

ELEVENTH HOUSE

This can be a very depressing time or a period of great joy, depending on how you have dealt with crisis in previous years. One area that will go through tests is that of friendships. At least one long-term friendship will end now and you may be saying goodbye to some superficial people too. Your social life is not exactly swinging now. If you worked hard when Saturn was in the tenth house, you will feel as if you've truly been rewarded by the time Saturn reaches the eleventh. I don't think Saturn is too much of a challenge here. You'll have some minor problems or adjustments, but I have found this is the house to worry least about when Saturn transits.

Lesson: The dynamics and relationships within your friendship circle and other groups. Letting go of negative people and perhaps depression.

How To Deal With This: Know that some friends may be leaving your life, but new ones will be coming in. You've learned all you can from certain people and it's time to move on. Shake any lethargy and depression.

TWELFTH HOUSE

When Saturn reaches the twelfth house, you feel a desire to go inward. You want to spend time alone. A period of life is over and you will begin a new one shortly. Since the twelfth house is also related to karma, you'll be rewarded or punished for deeds and efforts of the past 15 years. If you did something good for someone, there'll be a blessing of some sort, but if you've done something negative, this is the period in which you must pay the piper.

Subconscious issues from childhood or years past may bubble to the surface and one must deal with them. You can't shrug them off. So this is a good time for counseling. You'll need someone to help you deal with these deep psychological issues. You could be depressed now and want to shut the world out. People from the past (ones you really don't want to see) may come back into your life. You could have to deal with prisons, sick people, hospitals and the like. These dealings may not be favorable. Rather, they prove to be burdensome in some way.

Lesson: Karmic issues, letting go and the feeling of isolation

How to Deal with This: Don't lock yourself in a room. Force yourself outside and deal with others. Go to counseling now. Spend some time getting to know who you are!

As with any Saturn transit, some lesson is learned and something is taken way that has outlived its usefulness. Your life will be dramatically changed because of a Saturn transit either consciously or subconsciously. These are lessons your soul has chosen to learn in this lifetime. By knowing what the lessons are ahead of time, you can look at them from a spiritual perspective. If you fight the energy of Saturn and work against it, it will push harder. It is here to teach you, to change life for the better. But many people realize this only after the transit has passed. When Saturn hits a certain house in your chart, be open to what it is bringing you. Look for the reason behind the change or the challenge. What am I to learn? How can I grow from this lesson? Once you learn it, the great teacher Saturn will reward you. At the same time you are experiencing a Saturn transit, you are getting help from other planets. I always look for the helper or the planet that brings you support and "takes the edge off". There usually *is* one. Yes, your world will change because of Saturn. In time to come, life will be better for it too.

FOUR

Full Moons, New Moons, Eclipses Working with the Lunar Cycle

If you learn to work with the phases of the moon, you will avoid a lot of frustrations and headaches. You'll also be able to create a lot of opportunities. It's like being at the right place at the right time.

If you're going to schedule a project that will require a great deal of energy and enthusiasm, schedule it in the 2-week period between the new and full moon. Then, you will find that everything runs smoothly and falls in place easily. If you are going to finalize projects or add finishing touches, the 2 weeks between the full moon and the new moon are advantageous. This is a time that energy is at its lowest point and new beginnings of any kind are not highly favored.

MOON PHASES

The New Moon (first quarter)
—Good for new beginnings

Waxing Moon (second quarter)
—Projects are close to being completed.

Full Moon (third quarter)
—Results of our actions come to light.

No Moon (fourth quarter)
—Just learn. Keep silent. Plan for the next phase.

Moon Cycles

The moon is the fastest-traveling planet in our solar system. It moves into a new zodiac sign about every 2? days. Because the moon influences our emotional side, our moods and attitudes reflect the sign the moon is in on a particular day.

There are days when our lives run smoothly, and other days nothing goes right—when you're sorry you even got out of bed in the morning. If we follow the flow of the moon and understand its benefits, we can certainly fine tune our daily routine to run smoother. To know which sign the moon is in each day, you can buy an ephemeris that charts the daily movements of the planets, or buy a moon calendar; I offer one every year. My clients know when the full and new moon occurs and which sign the moon is in each day. There's information at the end of this chapter if you'd like to order one. For now, let's gain an understanding of how to utilize the moon to the greatest advantage.

A new moon occurs 2 weeks before a full moon. On a new moon, you should ask questions, start new projects or go on a job interview. Things you start on a new moon will come to completion on a full moon.

Full moons are when things often come to light. You'll get your answers. The full moon shines light on hidden agendas. Secrets come out. Answers are given. Jobs are offered. If you are waiting for something to happen, it should materialize by the full moon.

Full moons also are known to make people more anxious, supersensitive, and to force them to take action. You often hear about hideous crimes committed when the moon is full. Hospital emergency rooms are busier than usual and people in general are prone to act irrationally.

Cancer born people are ruled by the moon, so its energy affects them dramatically. Therefore, they are psychic, sensitive, emotional and react more to the energy of the moon now than at any other time of the month. A woman's menstruation cycle often coincides with the full moon too. More babies are born.

I know a manager, at a hotel conference center where I hold my seminars, who fired four long-term employees all in one day. I was talking to the girl at the front desk and asked, "Did this happen on a full moon?" She looked at the calendar and confirmed that, indeed, there had been a full moon! I remember waiting forever for a check from my book distributor. Finally, I gave up worrying about it after I realized I'd get paid on the full moon. It arrived the day before. By the way, the energy of the full moon is in effect 3 days before it actually becomes full and three days after. You will feel the effect more strongly as it becomes full, then feel it decrease during the following 3 days. So, if you are upset and don't know why, experience unusual bouts of anxiety, if people are grumpy and irrational, look at the calendar. We're probably close to a full moon!

As I stated earlier, about every 2? days, the moon changes from one zodiac sign to another. Each day, the moon exerts an influence over us. Because of the moon's placement, there are particularly good days to do things and other days you should avoid certain activities. Let's take a look at the themes for each moon day.

The Moon in the Signs

ARIES MOON

It's a great time to begin new projects and be a pioneer! Just make sure you follow through, days later. You tend to be more impulsive and ready to spring into action! You won't have much patience. New experiences could be a big part of this period. People may seem more bossy, selfish or pushy too. There is an increased amount of optimism.

TAURUS MOON

It's a good time to deal with money and investments, renting property and hiring new employees. Plant flowers and gardens. You will appreciate the finer things in life. This is a fertile period when ideas and projects begin to take root and grow. Many people you come in contact with are more stubborn and set in their ways. Good food becomes important. This is a fine time to prepare a home-cooked meal or go out for gourmet dining. On these days, you will be feeling more materialistic as well.

GEMINI MOON

Yakety-yak! Lots of communications, short trips and travel may be featured over the next 2 days when the moon is in Gemini. Your phone rings a lot and your mailbox is filled. You could be more creative in your writing and communication now. There's a tendency to be fickle, changing your mind quickly. You'll be on the run a lot, but the pace will slow in a few days. It's a great time to get out and play, be with friends, communicate your feelings and spend time with children.

CANCER MOON

Your home and family will be important when the moon is in Cancer. You just want to hang out around the house. You may feel more sentimental now than at other times and perhaps even more emotional and insecure. It's a good time to plan family get-togethers and even clean the house! You'll be more intuitive and imaginative these few days. Sometimes you may feel a little down because the moon in Cancer makes you deal with deep feelings you've been too busy to examine. It can be a nurturing time when you seek out things that make you feel safe and comfortable. Preparing comfort foods like macaroni and cheese, meat loaf and mashed potatoes are favorable. People want to nest.

LEO MOON

You're in the spotlight! People have more energy! This is a good time to throw a party. It's a great time to shop, because you will run into some super sales! Gambling increases now. People want to have fun, get out of the house and enjoy life! Romance, love and affairs of the heart seem to be a big theme. Your approach to life will be stronger and more ambitious. Watch out for people with big egos. At the same time, you may also meet many people with generous hearts. You may be very giving at this time too.

VIRGO MOON

These are workdays, when completing daily tasks becomes important. I find when moon is in Virgo I want everything in my house to be in perfect order. I'm more fussy about how things look and feel. These are the days to attend to detail and get errands caught up. It's a good time to work on health issues and make doctor appointments. People are more practical, fussy and have specific game plans for these days. It's a great time for getting good gossip too!

LIBRA MOON

More of a peaceful attitude persists when the moon moves into the sign of Libra. People need and want to be together. Relationships and their importance are magnified. Most people you meet during this period will be helpful, cooperative and tolerant. It is also a time to appreciate beauty, art, music and flowers. Play some of your favorite soothing music; buy some roses for your coffee table or office. Spend time with someone you love. Talk about a business partnership arrangement. Use this day for negotiating when everyone wants to "work things out".

SCORPIO MOON

This is a very intense time. It's a time for deep reflection and for getting 'to the bottom" of things. It's also great for sex. Be careful of jealousy and revengeful acts. People seem to be more private and skeptical. They reflect more on inner issues. Many want their privacy. It's a great time for regeneration, for breaking down worn-out patterns and rebuilding on a more solid structure. Book a psychic reading now, or delve into the occult.

SAGITTARIUS MOON

People are more optimistic and outgoing. This is a good day to travel long distance and deal with people of different cultures or religions. Folks will be honest and direct. It's not a good time to go shopping, because you may overspend and regret it later. However, it's a fine day to participate in sports or physical work. Education, travel and studying higher philosophy are all favored. Overall, there is general feeling of enthusiasm but a tendency to overindulge in things.

CAPRICORN MOON

A Capricorn moon favors getting things organized. It is a logical, precise time. People are more realistic and sometimes more cautious. Business and job related themes are highlighted. Folks tend to speak their mind, and opinions are very strong at this time. This is not an emotional, sensitive period. At times you may feel like these days are mundane. People tend to save their money. They are thriftier. Do not buy shoes under this moon; they'll hurt your feet later on!

AQUARIUS MOON

Expect the unexpected. Have no game plan. Just see what these few days bring and have to offer. The moon in Aquarius is great for surrounding yourself with friends, building a website and buying new technological gadgets. There is interest in community pride and doing things for the betterment of society. Unique ideas and opportunities may arise. A great day for group meetings, fundraisers and political events. People are more freedom oriented and don't want to be tied down.

PISCES MOON

A highly intuitive few days. You may have enlightening, bizarre dreams that force you to look at the deeper meaning of life. You may encounter whiny, anxious people or perhaps some very creative, giving folks. It is a time many feel guilty or emotional. It's also a period when people want to "escape" the harsh realities of the world. Be careful of drinking too much when there is a Pisces moon or of using drugs. People want to be more helpful now. It's a great time for seeing a romantic movie, having a candlelit dinner and getting lost in a daydream!

Moon Tips: Here are a few other tidbits that you may find interesting when working with the energy of the moon.

Tip for Choosing the Sex of Your Child

Studies have been done for years using the moon calendar for conception. There is a 92% accuracy rate in using this method for picking the sex of your child. If you conceive when the moon is in a feminine sign, you'll have a girl. If the moon is in a masculine sign, you'll have a boy. The feminine signs are: Taurus, Cancer,

Virgo, Scorpio, Capricorn and Pisces. The masculine signs are Aries, Gemini, Leo, Libra, Sagittarius and Aquarius.

Health Tips

You should never schedule surgery on a full moon. There is usually a complication, infection or something doesn't go right. The full moon is in effect 3 days before and 3 days after the night the moon is full. I always tell my clients to be careful around the entire week. Also never schedule an operation when the moon is in the same sign as your natal moon at birth. If you'd don't know what your moon is in, consult an astrologer or an ephemeris. It is a good idea to buy health insurance under a waxing moon in Taurus, Virgo or Scorpio. A medical exam will go well when the moon is waxing in Leo or Aries.

Do Not Have Surgeries or procedures done on these moon days in these specific areas:

Aries—Head, face

Taurus—Neck, throat

Gemini—Hands, lungs, wrists

Cancer—Breasts, stomach

Leo—Heart, back

Virgo—Intestines, stomach, pancreas

Libra—Bladder, kidney, forearm

Scorpio—Reproductive organs

Sagittarius—Hip, thighs and lower back

Capricorn—Knees

Aquarius—Ankles, calves

Pisces—Feet, eyes

Tips for Diets and Addictions

I tell people to start a diet on a new moon. If you can successfully stay on the program until the full moon, you will have gained discipline to further the weight loss. To stop an addiction, quit after the full moon in Pisces. You can kick a drinking problem or food addiction after the full moon in Taurus or Libra.

Tips for Intuitive Readings

If you're hoping to get an excellent psychic reading or just want to be able to tap into your own intuition, the days around and of the full moon are the most favorable. People are much more sensitive around this time, especially the water signs: Pisces, Cancer and Scorpio. Also book a reading on Pisces, Scorpio and Cancer moon days.

Tips on Void of Course Moon

When the moon is moving from one sign to another, sometimes it stops in between signs and takes a rest. It doesn't reach its new destination for a few hours or so. When the moon is not in any sign, this is called a void moon. Nothing ever happens on a void moon. Therefore, you should not plan a conference, party or anything important then. It's as if the world shuts down. People stop what they're doing. The energy of those few minutes or hours can bring a halt to everything. Nothing gets done. When I plan a seminar or expo, we may be very busy all morning and if a moon void hits around 11a.m. our attendance drops dramatically. No one comes through the door. People don't feel like going out. It's strange but it happens. Plan around moon voids.

Maria's Moon Void Tip—File your income taxes on a moon void. You won't be audited!

Moon Days for Each Sun Sign

The moon travels into a new zodiac sign every 2½ days. It influences the physical energy of the signs in different ways. Following is a guide you can use to understand high- and low-energy days, based on your zodiac sign.

ARIES

Monthly Peak—Aries Moon Days

Monthly Low—Libra Moon Days

Good Days—Aries, Leo and Sagittarius Moon Days

Irritating Days—Cancer, Capricorn Moon Days

TAURUS

Monthly Peak—Taurus Moon Days

Monthly Low—Scorpio Moon Days

Good Energy Days—Capricorn and Virgo Moon Days

Irritating Days—Aquarius and Leo Moon Days

GEMINI

Monthly Peak—Gemini Moon Days

Monthly Low—Sagittarius Moon Days

Good Energy Days—Aquarius and Libra Moon Days

Irritating Days—Pisces and Virgo Moon Days

CANCER

Monthly Peak—Cancer Moon Days
Monthly Low—Capricorn Moon Days
Good Energy Days—Pisces and Scorpio Moon Days
Irritating Days—Aries and Libra Moon Days

Note: Cancers are especially affected by the moon's movement.

LEO

Monthly Peak—Leo Moon Days
Monthly Low—Aquarius Moon Days
Good Energy Days—Aries and Sagittarius Moon Days
Irritating Days—Taurus and Scorpio Moon Days

VIRGO

Monthly Peak—Virgo Moon Days
Monthly Low—Pisces Moon Days
Good Energy Days—Taurus and Capricorn Moon Days
Irritating Days—Gemini and Sagittarius Moon Days

LIBRA

Monthly Peak—Libra Moon Days
Monthly Low—Aries Moon Days
Good Energy Days—Gemini and Aquarius Moon Days
Irritating Days—Capricorn and Cancer Moon Days

SCORPIO

Monthly Peak—Scorpio Moon Days
Monthly Low—Taurus Moon Days

Good Energy Days—Pisces and Cancer Moon Days
Irritating Days—Aquarius and Leo Moon Days

SAGITTARIUS

Monthly Peak—Sagittarius Moon Days
Monthly Low—Gemini Moon Days
Good Energy Days—Aries and Leo Moon Days
Irritating Days—Pisces and Virgo Moon Days

CAPRICORN

Monthly Peak—Capricorn Moon Days
Monthly Low—Cancer Moon Days
Good Energy Days—Taurus and Virgo Moon Days
Irritating Days—Aries and Libra Moon Days

AQUARIUS

Monthly Peak—Aquarius Moon Days
Monthly Low—Leo Moon Days
Good Energy Days—Gemini and Libra Moon Days
Irritating Days—Taurus and Scorpio Moon Days

PISCES

Monthly Peak—Pisces Moon Days
Monthly Low—Virgo Moon Days
Good Energy Days—Cancer and Scorpio Moon Days
Irritating Days—Gemini and Sagittarius Moon Days

Moon Activities

Try the following activities under certain moon days for the best results

Go fishing—Cancer, Pisces Moon

Throw a party—Leo, Libra Moon

Play sports—Sagittarius Moon

Competitive sports—Aries Moon

Travel—Gemini, Sagittarius Moon

Boating—Cancer Moon

Writing—Gemini Moon

Open a business—Capricorn Moon

Buying antiques—Cancer Moon

Buying stock—Taurus, Capricorn Moon

Mail letters—Gemini, Virgo Moon

Move—Taurus, Leo, Scorpio, Aquarius Moon

Beauty appointment—Taurus, Libra Moon

Borrow money—Leo, Sagittarius Moon

Buy a car—Gemini, Sagittarius Moon

Buy a home—Cancer, Taurus Moon

Get teeth pulled—Gemini, Virgo Moon

Cut hair for growth—Cancer, Pisces on a New Moon

Cut hair to retard hair growth—Aries, Gemini, Virgo Moon

Gain weight—Cancer, Pisces Moon

Get married—Taurus, Cancer, Leo, Libra, Pisces Moon

If you don't have a moon calendar, the bookstores are usually full of them by November. They sell out rather quickly. I produce one every year and information can be obtained by visiting my website www.MariaShaw.com or writing P.O. Box 490 Genesee, MI 48437.

Eclipses

WHAT IS AN ECLIPSE?

Eclipses shake up our lives. Most people are aware of an impending eclipse only if the TV weatherman points it out. But eclipses are more than just a phenomenon in the sky. The position, degree and sign an eclipse occurs in, will tell us what kind of affect it will have on us personally.

Yes, there are good and bad eclipses. I really shouldn't use the word "bad". Maybe "tough" is a better choice. Because in some way, shape or form, all eclipses have a positive effect on us anyway. Sometimes an eclipse causes energy that creates crisis in our lives. Through that crisis, we grow or complete something.

Eclipses push us off the fence. We cannot be indecisive any longer about an issue or decision when an eclipse is near. Say, for instance, that you hated your job but couldn't quit because you didn't have another lined up. You were miserable and knew you should look elsewhere for employment. An eclipse's energy could create challenges in your position. You could get fired. The company might file for bankruptcy. You may be forced out. The result would likely be a better job and a happier you!

I recall a former reader I employed, who refused to move out of the apartment she had rented for 10 years. She was a triple Capricorn, and you know how strong-willed Capricorn can be! Well, the landlords raised her rent. She refused to move. The area around her was depreciating and not considered as safe as it once was. At work, her department was being moved to a new location, farther away from her home. Still, she wouldn't budge. Asbestos was found in the apartment complex. Many tenants relocated. She did not. Then an eclipse came. The ceiling in her apartment caved in one day, forcing her to move out . . . temporarily. The Capricorn lady figured she'd move back in once the ceiling was repaired. The landlord told her she was out of luck. He wouldn't renew her lease. She was forced to move! Eventually, she found a cute, affordable condo. It was cheaper than rent, closer to work and she was building equity.

This is a good example of how an eclipse nudges us along. It's as if the hand of fate is pushing us. By this time you don't have a choice. The ability to make your own decision is taken away from you.

Eclipses bring a change of status; death, birth, endings, relocation and new relationships. Yet, nothing happens on an eclipse that hasn't already begun. The handwriting was on the wall weeks and even months before. The wheels of motion had already started turning. That's why I tell clients, they'll get some sort of preview of what an eclipse is bringing beforehand. If you're constantly arguing with your boyfriend, when an eclipse hits, it could create a breakup. If you're considering suing someone, the first court date may be on an eclipse. If one falls on or close to your birthday, the following year of your life will be very interesting, exciting and climactic.

One important thing to remember is that you should never "act" or make decisions on an eclipse. Listen first to what the universe is telling you and then respond accordingly. You may not have all of the facts. Do not initiate. Do not jump to conclusions or rush into anything. Sit back and wait until the eclipse has run its course; then proceed. The aftermath of an eclipse usually occurs within 3 weeks to 3 months. Others astrologers claim it takes an entire year for the drama to play out. I have noticed that most of the energy occurs 90 days after and 3 weeks before.

Sometimes an eclipse can be troublesome to a person's health because of the disruption in solar energy. A friend's father had a stroke on the eclipse in June 2002. My father died on an eclipse in

1997. So did Princess Diana and Mother Teresa. The plane of John F. Kennedy Jr. went down on another. You always hear of tragic events taking place around this time. That's because the media reports only tragedy and crisis. But many good things happen on eclipses, as well. I landed a great television position on an eclipse. Good news floods in. There's a flurry of calls, letters and communication. Eclipses bring what is needed—like a promotion or a proposal, a new idea perhaps. There's important news coming that can change your life.

If your lover says they're leaving you on an eclipse, they mean it! It's no joke. If you hear a rumor around an eclipse, it's probably true. Listen up! Sometimes, eclipses bring subtle news and mysterious messages that take patience and time to figure out. You get bits and pieces of information. More details come as time passes. That's why you shouldn't take action or make rash decisions until all of the news is out.

An eclipse occurs about every 5½ months, and the same eclipse (in the same sign) returns every 19 years. A new moon eclipse is gentler than a full moon eclipse, which brings everything to a head. People born under the sign of Leo are the most affected by solar eclipses because the sun is their ruling planet. Those born under the sign of Cancer are affected by lunar eclipses because they are ruled by the moon. Solar eclipses affect the men in your life and the lunar ones affect female relationships as well as the home and family. If you go for a mammogram or medical test on an eclipse and something shows up on the X-ray, follow up right away and go for more testing. To find out exactly how an eclipse will affect you, consult a professional astrologer a few months before an eclipse is expected. You can prepare yourself for the events that may unfold. If you understand astrology, look at the sign and the degree of the eclipse and see what house it falls in, in your chart. Also, look for other planets it may aspect.

ECLIPSE DATES—2003–2010

Maria's Eclipse Tip—If you were born on a new moon eclipse, you will be lucky!

May 15, 2003

May 30, 2003

November 8, 2003

November 23, 2003

April 19, 2004

May 4, 2004

October 14, 2004

October 28, 2004

April 8, 2005

April 24, 2005

October 3, 2005

October 17, 2005

March 14, 2006

March 29, 2006

September 7, 2006

September 22, 2006

March 3, 2007

March 19, 2007

August 28, 2007

September 11, 2007

February 7, 2008

February 21, 2008

August 1, 2008

August 16, 2008

January 26, 2009

February 9, 2009

July 7, 2009

July 22, 2009

August 6, 2009

December 31, 2009

January 15, 2010

FIVE

Mercury Retrograde— Friend or Foe?

"Mercury retrograde" is quickly becoming a buzz phrase these days. We're hearing it on morning-drive radio, around the water cooler and even among new age "non-believers".

What exactly is a Mercury retrograde? My clients know. I've been preaching to them for years . . . telling them how to work through these periods, or work around them!

In astrology, the planet Mercury rules communication, travel, contracts, automobiles and the written word. It goes in a retrograde motion (backwards) three times a year for approximately 3 weeks at a time. When Mercury is retrograde, there's a lot of confusion. People forget things. There are delays and frustrations.

You should never start anything new when Mercury goes retrograde. But you can still put this astrological aspect to good use.

You need to learn to work with the energy of Mercury rather than against it.

In this chapter, we'll explore the pros and cons of this cosmic force. You'll learn how to work with Mercury retrogrades and how to prepare yourself for the days and times the planet goes forward or "direct".

There is usually a "wind up" period 2 weeks before Mercury goes retrograde. This is a time to finalize the business at hand. When the dreaded day arrives, you should have finished all of your projects that are important.

I have a few stories to share with you about Mercury retrogrades. I had a rental house that I needed to rent ASAP. It was costing me money to leave it empty. Of course I was anxious to get someone moved in. My realtor did background and credit checks on all of the applicants. We found what I thought was a great, capable young couple. I knew I should never sign contracts on a retrograde, but I was impatient. I couldn't and wouldn't wait a month longer to sign a lease. The couple eagerly signed on the dotted line. I kept my fingers crossed. The next month, their rent was 2 weeks late. Two months later, they trashed the place, illegally placed bills in my name, moved out with no notice and filed for bankruptcy so we couldn't sue them. From that moment on, I promised myself I would never sign another contract on a Mercury retrograde and I never have.

Years before this incident and before I even knew what a Mercury retrograde was, I had wanted to buy a home. My husband and I made an offer on this wonderful place during a June Mercury retrograde. The offer was declined. We asked for a counter offer. None was forthcoming. The realtors couldn't hook up with the owners. There was a lot of miscommunication. The homeowners left the state on vacation for a few weeks. It took us until

October to get a response and finally, a "yes", after re-writing the original offer three times!

My friend and fellow astrologer Cindy should have known better. She started a new job on the first day Mercury went retrograde. She asked me how I felt the new position would go. "You won't stay there." I told her. It's a Mercury retrograde." The next day she quit!

This same gal actually had a lot of nerve trying to tempt fate. She went out and bought a new car on another retrograde. It broke down on the expressway on the drive home from the dealer. It stayed parked in her garage until Mercury went direct. It was weeks before her car problems were solved. Her excuse for buying on a Mercury retrograde? Her husband was buying the car and she didn't want him to back out of the offer!

Now, you can't stop your life just because a Mercury retrograde rolls around. There are things you can't avoid or put off. But if you do have time to plan ahead, you can save yourself a lot of headaches.

One thing I tell my clients, is that you should never get married on a Mercury retrograde or a Venus retrograde for that matter. You will never "feel" married. Sometimes the unions don't last more than a year.

Because mercury also rules travel and trips, it is not a good time to travel unless you have backup plans. Expect delays, double-check your hotel accommodations beforehand (and the day of) and clarify everything with everyone.

I booked a cruise for my husband's 40th birthday. It wasn't a Mercury retrograde when I booked the trip but the ship was set to sail during one of those crazy times. We went to the airport to fly to Florida. The gate agent told us the trip was canceled. The ship had caught on fire! So we drove to Canada instead for a long weekend. Our trip was cut short when relatives called and told us to hurry home—there had been an emergency in the family!

Sometimes, even when you plan ahead, Mercury retrograde can get the best of you! My friends and I were heading to the airport to catch a flight to New Orleans. I told Sherry to meet me at my house half an hour earlier than usual, so we wouldn't be late. She left her house early but missed the turn to my road and went 30 minutes out of her way! Once she had picked me up and we'd made it to the freeway, there was a 6-mile traffic back-up because of road construction. We made it through that. However, because we started late, we ended up in Detroit's morning rush-hour traffic and were delayed again. I was doing 90 miles an hour to get to the airport and it looked like we'd actually make the flight. Then the tire on my car blew! Luckily someone stopped to help, but we were about 7 minutes late getting to the gate and had to take a later flight.

Three hours later, we boarded a plane scheduled to leave at 12:20 p.m. A contract worker had left a crane sitting in front of the plane. He went to lunch. No one could locate him and our flight was stuck until he came back. . . . half an hour later!

Some Don'ts and Do's

DON'T

—Start anything new
—Make important decisions
—Buy computers, appliances, TVs, radios, etc.
—Travel without back-up plans
—Sign contracts

—Buy a car
—Expect things to move quickly
—Take anything for granted
—Negotiate a contract
—File a lawsuit
—Start a new job
—Begin a new class
—Go on a "first" date

WHAT YOU CAN EXPECT

—Angrier people
—Crazy drivers
—More accidents
—Miscommunication
—Quarrels
—Computer problems and breakdowns
—Delays
—More mistakes
—Slow mail
—Playing phone tag
—Wrong directions
—Missed appointments
—Dead cell phone batteries

Anything you start will have to be re-done or revised. If you begin a big project during one of these periods, it will go over budget and take longer than expected.

What is Mercury Retrograde Good For?

If you understand the cycles of Mercury retrograde, which appears about every 3 months, you can work *with*, rather than *against* the flow of Mercury's energy.

Remember the "re" in retrograde. These weeks are good for re-doing just about anything.

DO

—Re-apply for a job

—Re-do hair color

—Re-write your resume

—Review your bank account

—Renew a loan

—Repair your car

—Re-contact past clients

—Research

Catch up on all of the mundane work and tasks you set aside, and also have a game plan in place for when Mercury goes direct. It's a super time to finish up and clean up too!

Mercury retrograde is also used to reflect on what you've accomplished thus far and where you want to redirect your energies. There are those "re" words again! We all need time to review and decide whether we're on the right path. These weeks give us the opportunity to do so.

My first book was written before Mercury went retrograde. During the "retro" I reviewed and re-edited it. That process went well and I found mistakes I had missed months before.

Years ago, I worked as a television newscaster. I left the station for a few years and returned, hoping to get my old job back. I was *re*-hired during a Mercury retrograde!

As I mentioned earlier, we can't stop our lives every time a retrograde hits. So what can you do when you don't have a choice? Have some chocolate! Just kidding. You may have to start a new job or file court papers during a Mercury retrograde. Here's a list, to make things a little easier . . .

What To Do If You Can't Postpone or Delay Activity

—Read and re-read contracts. Have someone else look them over too.

—Check your travel plans several times.

—Ask questions over and over, if you need to, during negotiations.

—Mail packages and letters early. Check the zip codes.

—Fill your gas tank.

—Don't check luggage when you're flying. Carry on everything, if you can.

—If you are making purchases, keep your sales receipts and know the stores' return policies.

—Keep your cell phone battery charged.

—Watch your driving.

There are some people who never seem to be affected during this period. Chances are that they were born when Mercury was retrograde. Millions of people are born during these times. How do these weeks affect them? Well, Mercury retrograde babies thrive. Things appear easier for them and run smoothly. They get the new job, start building the new house and travel to Las Vegas. It's okay to push forward in the outside world. If you're one of these people, you'll have the edge on everyone else! How do you find out? Your astrology chart will indicate whether Mercury was retrograde when you were born.

MERCURY RETROGRADE CALENDAR

2003
January 2–January 23
April 26–May 20
August 28–September 20
December 17–January 6

2004
December 17, 2003–January 6
April 6–April 30
Aug 10–September 2
November 30–December 20

2005
March 20–April 12
July 23–August 16
November 14–December 4

2006
March 2–March 25
July 4–July 29
October 28–November 18

2007
February 14–March 8
June 15–July 10
October 12–November 1

2008
January 28–February 19
May 26–June 19
September 24–October 15

2009
January 11–February 1
May 7–May 31
September 7–September 29
December 26–January 15, 2010

2010
April 18–May 11
August 20–September 12
December 10–December 30

Hopefully, this chapter provides you with enough information to keep your life running smoothly. I suggest keeping a journal of what happens to you during the retrograde periods. Remember to plan and work with Mercury. Think of retrogrades as time-outs. They can be very beneficial to you when used correctly.

SIX

The Solar Return

★ ★ ★ Every year, on or around your birthday, you have a sacred moment that you should be aware of and ready for. This special moment is called your "solar return". It occurs when the sun comes back to the exactly the same placement as when you were born, to join the earth. This does not happen the same time every year but can happen the day before, on and even the day after your birthday.

Why is this moment so special? Why is knowing the time it occurs so important? There is a special power that is released into the universe during this magic moment that can help you take control of your own fate and destiny. Through the power of your mind, your desire and intent, you can manifest great things. It sounds so easy. It sounds too good to be true. But there is a process to it. You need to learn it so you can seize this power and claim it for your own. This is one moment in which you can control what happens over the course of the next year. You can't be late. You must be right on time and you must prepare accordingly.

To find your solar return time, you need to contact a professional astrologer and give them your birthday, time of birth and the city you were born in. The astrologer will also need to know where you plan to be on your next birthday. With this information, the astrologer will give you the exact time of your solar return. She can also use the solar return chart to forecast events and highlight the main theme of your upcoming year. With prior knowledge, you will know which areas of life will expand and which areas you should pay closer attention to.

Now Here's What You Do on Your Solar Return:

Ten minutes before your solar return begins, prepare yourself mentally, emotionally and physically. When the solar return occurs, you want to be happy, free of any worry or concern and be doing something you enjoy. Why? because this magical moment sets the stage for the next 12 months. Whatever happens then, however you feel, the frame of mind you're in, all will dictate how the year will progress. Therefore, you don't want to be arguing with your mate, feel depressed or have issues at work. Bad experiences or troubled feelings will set the tone for the entire year.

You can choose to handle your magical moment anyway you wish, but I have a few suggestions. At the very second your solar return occurs, you could be meditating, visualizing and affirming the way you want your new year to turn out. You should plan something special. You should feel empowered at this time, peaceful and happy. I don't care if you had a lousy day and hours before your car blew up. If you were arguing with your boss, forget it. If your lover dumped you, get over it! You must keep a positive thought pattern going for at least 10 minutes around the solar return time.

Location is important. If you can take the day off work and travel to a special place, by all means, do so. If you feel happiest feeding pigeons at the park, take your bread crumbs and go! Perhaps you like the beach. Maybe you just love being home. Go wherever you feel at peace and happy.

If you are home, you may want to surround yourself with things you treasure. My solar return was the night before my birthday one year. I listened to the *Somewhere In Time* CD and had a glass of nice wine while I sat on my front porch. I closed my eyes and visualized everything I wanted for the next year. In my mind, I went over my goals and objectives for my career. Spending more time at my vacation home was also on my wish list. I ran through all of my goals rather quickly in my mind and I affirmed that they would happen. I thanked God for all that He had already given me. It was perfect! I sat in my antique rocker and looked across the roads at the hayfields. The scent of garden flowers filled the air. I studied the "cotton candy" clouds that hovered overhead. I felt there was no place I would rather be in the world than on my porch that very moment.

You should plan to start your meditations 5 minutes before the solar return occurs and continue 5 minutes past it. Some people plan little rituals. They prepare a sacred space in which to meditate. They may pick flowers or burn incense. Some play their favorite music.

Other people plan this event to include people they love. A client of mine in Detroit had me do her solar return last year. She was given a time of 2:45 a.m. I told her she could set an alarm and do something special or just sleep through it. It was her choice. She decided to celebrate with her boyfriend. They went to dinner around 10 p.m., followed by dancing, and got cuddly about 2:30 a.m. I followed up with her to see how her first experience with the solar return went. "It was great! We had a wonderful time to-gether", she chuckled. And they've been having a wonderful time ever since!

If your solar return happens in the middle of the night and you do not plan to get up to greet it, I have a few suggestions. Before you go to bed that night, make sure your sheets and bedding are clean and comfortable. Wear some nice, new pajamas. Put flowers on your night stand. Play soft, relaxing music. Put a sweet scented sachet under your pillow. Make the sleeping hours as pleasant as possible. This doesn't mean you'll be sleeping through the next 12 months, but if you're relaxed and comfortable, rest assured you'll get your share of a good night's sleep.

You cannot be late for your solar return; otherwise, you will be late for everything over the next year.

The Solar Return Journal

Wait! There's more to this process. Over the course of your solar return day, events will unfold, interesting things could happen and unique people may come into your life. What happens over the course of the day, sets the tone for the upcoming year. The time these events occur will relate to a specific month over the next twelve months.

I suggest you keep a journal of everything that happens to you from the moment of your solar return through the following 24 hours—the more detail, the better. Keep a notebook handy at all times to write things down. Every 2-hour block of time represents a month in the upcoming year. Let's say your solar return occurred at 10 a.m. At 12 noon, whatever you are experiencing, could be symbolic of what will happen 1 month after your birthday. So 2 p.m. would represent 2 months after your birthday. And 4 p.m. represents 3 months. And so on. I suggest you plan ahead so that the hours following your solar return are happy times too. Spend time doing what you enjoy and with people who enrich your life.

I kept a journal and wrote down everything that happened over the course of the day. My friend spent part of the afternoon with me and she complained about her husband the entire time. I knew every time I'd see her over the next year, she would do the same. This was last June and as of this writing, almost a year later, she is still upset with him and I hear about it every time we get together!

Knowledge is power. You have control over your destiny if you have prior knowledge. You can get a solar return reading or report done to prepare you so you may influence the outcome of your day. Astrologers can explain what you may expect your new year to be like. It's a good idea to get the report done at least a month or two before your birthday. That way, you can change or prepare for issues that may show in the report.

If you don't like the aspects in the report, all you need to do is work with your astrologer on changing the location of where the solar return will take place. You may have to plan a vacation upstate or in another city to have the best possible aspects. If you are hoping to strengthen career opportunities, you may need to spend your solar return a few hours away rather than at home. If it's love your looking for, the aspects may be better in another direction. Decide what it is you wish to build on during the upcoming year and consult with an expert on the best locations to achieve maximum potential.

If you would like a report and don't know your exact birth time, but can estimate it within an hour, you can still have a report done. It will not be as accurate, so you'll have to increase the time you spend in harmony during the solar return. The solar return chart is a wonderful tool at your disposal to create positive experiences. Remember, astrologers can give you the aspects and the opportunity times that show in your chart, but only *you* have the power of free will to make wishes come true.

Worksheet for Your Solar Return

Date and Time of Solar Return _____

List some things you'd like to affirm and see happen over the course of the next year

Make your list here:

1.

2.

3.

4.

5.

6.

7.

8.

9.

10.

Use another piece of paper if you have more to write.

Solar Return Journal

Start taking notes after the solar return occurs. For example, if your solar return was at 3p.m., start writing down activities and events that transpire around 4 p.m. Here's a handy format. Jot a few notes about what's going on in your life each hour. For example if you received an important business call, write it down. If you had a wonderful dinner with your friends, note it. This worksheet starts at midnight but please begin at the appropriate time of your solar return.

12 Midnight

_____

_____

_____

1.A.M.

_____

_____

_____

2 A.M.

_____

_____

_____

3 A.M.

_____

_____

_____

4 A.M.

_____

_____

_____

5 A.M.

_____

_____

_____

6 A.M.

_____

_____

_____

7 A.M.

_____

_____

_____

8 A.M.

_____

_____

_____

9 A.M.

_____

_____

_____

10 A.M.

_____
_____
_____

11 A.M.

_____
_____
_____

12 Noon

_____
_____
_____

1.P.M.

_____
_____
_____

2 P.M.

_____
_____
_____

3 P.M.

_____
_____
_____

4 P.M.

_____
_____
_____

5 P.M.

_____

_____

_____

6 P.M.

_____

_____

_____

7 P.M.

_____

_____

_____

8 P.M.

_____

_____

_____

9 P.M.

_____

_____

_____

10 P.M.

_____

_____

_____

11 P.M.

_____

_____

_____

Now, that you've finished your journal, refer back to it every month. You'll notice how similar themes play out over the course of the next year. This way, you'll know what to expect ahead of time. Predicting your own future can be fun!

The Earth Day

You understand now the magic a solar return holds. There's another precious time that can also help you realize your dreams and goals. It can aid in balance and grounding. We call it *The Earth Day*.

This is the one day of the year when the sun meets your personal "grounding point", which is a point of peace, harmony and balance. How do you find it? It's much simpler than locating the exact moment of your solar return. Here's an example: Your birthday is June 25th. Six months away from your birthday is your Earth Day. A person born on June 25th would celebrate their earth day on December 25th every year.

WHAT TO DO ON THE EARTH DAY

Your solar return was a time to plant seeds for a new year. The opposite point, Earth Day, is a time to see how well those seeds have taken sprout. You should ask yourself how your goals have progressed. Are your dreams sprouting or do they need to be re-rooted? Use The Earth Day to reflect on these questions and, if you need to, get back on track with your goals. This is a time a person can clearly see their objectives. You'll see the other side of the coin too. If one has gotten off path, it's time to regroup and make dreams a reality.

SEVEN

What Color "Aura" You?

Exploring Auras

Ever notice that when you first meet some people, you feel very comfortable around them? You immediately like them. You have good, warm, fuzzy feelings? Then on the other hand, there are people who make you feel uneasy to be around. You can't wait to say "adios" and be on your way! That's because some people drain your energy, while others add to it! These feelings happen because we are "sensing" another person's *energy field*, also known as an *aura*.

Think of an aura as a light fluffy cloud of cotton candy surrounding your entire body. It's invisible for the most part to the naked eye. But if you look closer, perhaps with your third eye, your intuitive higher side will see it. You may think only psychics see auras, but that's not true. Everyone can see an aura if they know what they are looking for. You're already sensing them! That's the feeling we described in the first paragraph.

You sense other people's energy every minute of the day. Let's say your friend comes over to visit. She's depressed about something. You'll sense it the minute she walks in the door.

"What's wrong?" you'll ask.
"Nothing." she'll say.
"I know something is up with you. Tell me!" you persist.

She finally gives in and tells you about her problem. You sensed her energy was down before she said anything. Likewise, you will know when she is excited or happy about something too.

How To Develop
Your Aura Readings Skills

First of all, you have to trust your intuition—that little "voice" in your head giving you messages or that "feeling" in the pit of your stomach. Clear your mind a little, take a few deep breaths, slow down your thinking. Listen to what you "feel". What are the first thoughts that come to mind? Notice how your body responds. Do you feel anxious, excited, confident or confused? It takes a little practice but you'll get it.

This ability is something everyone has. Some people just use it more than others. Some are scared of it. This is nothing to be frightened of. Intuition is "how you feel". Once you get in touch with and trust those feelings, you'll develop and use them more and more. Don't question your first thought. The problem with intuition is that most people try to analyze or second-guess it. Go with it! It won't serve you wrong. The more you use it, the more your psychic abilities grow.

You can use your intuition when reading someone's aura. Many people have confided in me that they've been seeing colors around others for years, ever since they were small children. This is not unusual. If you are one of these folks who already sees color, you are seeing auras! So, let's take this task a step further. Let's learn how to read auras!

There is a simple way to read an aura. Have a friend stand against a plain white wall with no distracting pictures or curtains. Shut off the lights or make sure the room is dark. Take a flashlight and shine it above your friend's head. Be careful not to shine it in his eyes! Concentrate on the middle of his forehead, between his eyes. Clear your mind. It may take a few seconds, but soon you should see soft, faint colors outlining his head, shoulders and arms, against the wall. Sometimes the colors will be vibrant and sometimes faint. The more you practice, the more you will see. Do *not* question whether you really saw a particular color.

At some point, you will see a white light around his body, as it's the most common color to have in the aura. He may have more than one color in his energy field, depending on what he is experiencing or feeling at the time. An aura can extend for several feet outward from the body if one is open and energetic. If your friend is tired or sad, the aura is apt to be smaller, harder to see—hugging his body closely. An aura extends from the top of the head, down the shoulders and legs, to the soles of the feet. It really does look like fluffy cotton candy or a fuzzy cloud.

Do you know someone who makes you smile when you're down? Just by hanging out with them, you feel happy and excited about life? This person is "extending" their aura. They probably have a large aura and are projecting it onto you. Those who make you feel tired and depressed may have weak auras and draw from your energy field. You may feel they are constantly pulling on you. You can't wait to get away. Most people don't mean to take energy and don't realize they are doing this.

There are times when we feel a need to touch someone who is hurting, either physically or emotionally. We are exchanging energy by choice. Let's say a small child fell off a bike and skinned her knee. You would immediately go to help her and offer a hug. You're letting your aura connect with hers so she'll feel better! This is a natural instinct.

Have you ever been alone in a room and felt someone was looking at you? You didn't hear anyone but just sensed something was there? You turned around and *there* someone was! You're sensing an aura! You're feeling energy.

Your aura changes according to what is going on around you. If one minute you're happy and energetic and the next you hear bad news, your aura can change in a spilt second. Even thoughts can change our energy. Think about a sad movie and you'll feel tired or lose energy. Now, erase that thought and think about someone you really love or a wonderful trip you took. You'll immediately feel the changes within. A trained eye can see the aura change instantly! It can be of a single color or many different colors.

The Meaning of Color

There are many different colors that show up in the auric field. They all have different meanings. Here's a list of the most basic colors you'll find when reading an aura.

PINK

Pink stands for love. If you see someone with a pinkish glow in their auric field, this is a good sign. This person is full of love and friendly vibrations. They are feeling good and are open to giving and receiving love.

GREEN

Green is a nice color to see around someone. It is a healing color. Many doctors and medical professionals have green in their aura. Green usually means someone is healthy and free from pain. If you see a heavy concentration of green around someone, it sometimes means that person was very sick but is now well!

BLUE

Blue is a color of peace and understanding. It has a calming effect. As a side note; if you can't sleep at night and you're tossing and turning, throw a pair of blue pajamas on or a blue blanket. Blue will help you relax. Don't wear red to bed. Red is the color of energy and will keep you up all night! Blue usually means someone is relaxed and feeling pretty good about life. You'll feel at ease around someone with a blue aura.

YELLOW

Yellow is the color of communication. Yakety-yak! If you have a yellow aura, bet on a flurry of phone calls, creative writing assignments, letters and e-mail. You'll be getting the latest gossip and talking up a storm yourself. Yellow is also good for mental concentration.

PURPLE

Purple around someone usually means they are very spiritual or that their psychic abilities are developing and expanding. These people are looking for a higher purpose in life and seek universal truth. They will be optimistic and positive. Purple in an aura can also mean lucky times are ahead!

RED

Red is the color of anger or energy. Red can mean a couple different things. If you sense it in someone's aura, take time to "feel" it. Does the red feel good or bad? Someone with a lot of red in their auric field will probably experience burn-out down the road. But if it is mixed with other colors, it can intensify the positive energies of those colors. Red also relates to sensuality. If you feel the red you see is too strong or it bothers you, that person may be guilty of stealing other people's energy. They could be angry too. Beware!

ORANGE

Orange is the color of joy! It brings energy and happiness. Someone with orange in their aura will make you feel alive and excited about life! They will find delight in simple things and are a pleasure to be around.

GOLD

Gold is one of the highest spiritual colors you can have. Many psychics and highly spiritual people will have gold in their energy fields. Gold is usually intermingled with other colors.

GRAY

Gray is not a good color to have in your aura. When I see gray in someone's energy field, I visualize a white light and a soft pink light around that person. Then I mentally visualize the healing color of green around them. I concentrate until the gray color lifts, fades and turns into one of the brighter colors. Gray usually means a person is tired or sick. It's not healthy and if left in the energy field for a long time, can affect the person in an adverse way.

WHITE

White is the white light of Christ, the power of protection. Most people have white in their aura. It is actually the first light to encircle their entire body. It brings peace, protection and balance.

Besides the colors of an aura, you will want to notice whether the aura is balanced on all sides. The color should be even all around the body, so the flow of energy is equal. Sometimes people's auras have holes in them. There may be gaps or breaks in the energy field. This is not good. People who are ill experience this. A healthy aura is one that is fairly well extended, vibrates in a positive color and is balanced with no breaks in it's path.

How To Read Your Own Aura

AURA PHOTOGRAPHY

You've learned how to read auras and what the colors mean. However, reading your own aura can be quite difficult. But there is a way to see it . . . with the help of a camera. Yes, your aura can be captured on film. But not just with any old camera.

There are professional aura photographers who will take your picture with specialized cameras used just for this purpose. (These cameras cost about $10,000.) Most of these aura photographers can be found at new age expos. Their prices range from $10 for a snapshot to $25 for a photo with a printed report and interpretation.

You will sit in a chair and place your hands on a magnetic arm-rest connected by a cable to the camera. That magnet will pick up your energy field and the camera will interpret it as color. Strike your pose, smile and pouf, the photographer takes your picture!

The film is a lot like a Polaroid™ and you'll have to wait a few minutes for the picture to develop. Then you'll see colors all around your head, shoulders and arms. The aura photos are usually just head shots or photos taken from the waist up.

Because your aura changes, the photos also change each time you have one taken. The colors in your picture will tell a lot about your emotional state; whether you are happy or sad, worried or excited.

I had one client who had a lot of problems with her mother. She came in to get an aura photo done at one of my workshops. Her picture turned out all red, the color of anger. Months later, she came back to get another photo taken. She had been in therapy for several weeks and was working on emotional pain tied to her Mom. Her picture still had red in it, although, not as much. There were also shades of blue (understanding) and green (emotional healing). Several months went by and this young lady came back one more time to get her photo taken. She had finished therapy and was no longer angry with her mother. Her photo proved it! She had beautiful colors of blue, yellow and a great deal of pink (love) all around her! The aura camera had captured her mood, emotions, thoughts and feelings over the course of several months. It confirmed that she had worked through many problems and issues.

Auras can tell us a lot about how people are feeling and perhaps even the issues they are dealing with. Now, that you've learned a little more about the energy field, you can use color to help you feel better and boost vitality. Remember, seeing auras is not difficult. Like anything else, it just takes practice. I wish you all rainbows!

EIGHT

Chakras

★ ★ ★ So you're an expert aura reader now! But wait, there's more to learn. We have energy "points" in our body that affect our well being, too. These are called chakras (pronounced *shak-rahs*).

Our chakras open and close and can easily get out of "whack". When you feel tired or "out of balance", your chakras may not be working properly. We've all heard the saying "disease of the body is caused by dis-ease in the mind and spirit." For example, let's say someone violated you today. You were verbally abused and quite upset about it. Perhaps your mind can't stop thinking about the incident. So it doesn't rest. If your mind is disturbed, your body gets upset. You may get a stomach ache or not feel like eating. This is a good example of how emotions can affect our health. If you are ***really angry*** about something over a period of time, it will likely turn into a health condition; maybe back pain or migraine headaches.

It is said that a chest cold occurs because we fail to voice our opinion about a matter. We need to say something, tell someone off or speak up. *Translation: we need to get something off our chest.* Instead, to keep peace and harmony, we'll close our mouth, grin and bear it. Then our chest hurts or we develop congestion. We sometimes let others take advantage of us in hopes that they'll like us or give us approval. Under certain circumstances, that's okay. Every situation is different. But if we consistently let others make our decisions—if we vow to keep peace against our better judgment—if we allow others to control our actions, words and even our feelings—then we are asking for trouble with a capital T. We are allowing someone else to take our power away.

Let me tell you . . . you are the only person who can control the power someone has over you. Don't give that power away to anyone. Many times, we give away our personal power to people we really don't know all that well. Sometimes to our boss. Many times to our lover or spouse. Why do we do it? Often, we want people to like us. We want to avoid an argument. Most people think they're just being nice. But while you're busy trying to create all of this "niceness", someone is taking your personal power and draining your energy. You're stressed out and your spirit is low.

Stressed spelled backwards spells desserts
(Some of us overeat when we are stressed out)

We put food in our mouths to relieve stress, but what do we do to nourish our spirit? This chapter will show you how to claim and reclaim your own personal power . . . your spirituality. Remember if the mind is unsettled, the body can't rest—and nothing is in balance if the spirit is not alive and empowered. You need to believe that you are the only person who can control your own happiness and inner peace. To believe this is to become empowered. Keeping that power and positive energy flowing throughout the body is important. How do we do this? By balancing our chakras.

So, let's talk about chakras. Chakras are the energy points in our body. We have hundreds, maybe even thousands, but you're only to be concerned with the seven main ones now. The energy points can be wide open or completely shut down. When chakras are up and running—operating properly—we feel at peace, vivacious and alive. When they're shut down or closed for long periods, we feel depressed and tired.

Each energy point vibrates to certain colors, crystals and gemstones. Each defines a certain part of the body. Knowing what each chakra's responsibility is, helps us understand what is lacking or working in our life. For example, if the heart chakra is shut down, we may need to be more open to love. Perhaps we are hurting over a breakup in a relationship. If the heart chakra is healthy, we are able to give and receive the power of love endlessly.

Sometimes, when we experience emotional or physical pain, we subconsciously shut down our chakras. Maybe we'll shut just one down. Some will not work at all, and others may be operating at only a 50 percent level.

We block our energy, too, by suppressing feelings, depleting our physical energy, not getting enough sleep and denying our feelings. Now that you know a little more about chakras, let's take a look at each of the seven chakras, individually, and discover their purpose. The following information may give you clues about which of your chakras are working properly and those that need more attention.

The Root Chakra

The first chakra is the root chakra (grounding chakra). It starts at the base of the spine and runs near the pelvic bones.

Color—Red
Crystal/Gem—Garnet
Rules—The physical body

If the root chakra is damaged or not functioning properly, the other chakras will not work. All will be shut down. You will feel unbalanced.

When you were born, the chakras were developed in a rough form. The root chakra undergoes its major development in the first few weeks and months of life. Childhood trauma can do severe damage to the root chakra. Throughout later years, one may feel they are just going through the motions of life. They have a tendency to feel lonely and as if they don't belong. Some people who have damaged the root chakra, will try to escape the everyday world, by using drugs, eating too much or becoming obsessed with work. Others just feel tired all of the time.

Think of the root chakra as your *foundation*. If the foundation is weak, other parts of you may crumble. A balanced and healthy root chakra will provide you with much energy and vitality. You'll be excited about life. You'll feel grounded, sleep better and experience less stress.

The Sacral Chakra

The second chakra is the sacral or sex chakra. It rules the area below the belly button.

Color—Orange
Crystal/Gem—Carnelian
Rules—Our emotional side

While our root chakra is about our foundation, the sacral or sex chakra is about sexuality and the balance between our feminine and masculine sides. Our masculine side, also known as the left side of our brain, deals with logic, ambition and male oriented issues. Our feminine side or right brain makes us aware of our creative, emotional and intuitive nature.

After attaining a balanced and healthy sex chakra, a person feels like they've "got it all together". They'll feel affectionate towards others. They'll enjoy an active and healthy sex life.

If the sex chakra is blocked, some people lose the ability to nurture others and won't even accept a hug if it's offered. Some avoid relationships and commitments with others at all costs. The sex chakra can be completely shut down if there was sexual abuse. Sexual dysfunction is also common.

When the sacral chakra is open, you will not feel blocked or tired. One feels bursts of energy and creativity. There is a increase in enthusiasm for life and much more self confidence. You'll feel sexy and as if you can conquer the world!

The Solar Plexus

The Solar Plexus is the third chakra. It can be found above the stomach, in the gut. It's what I call your gut feeling.

Color—Yellow
Crystal/Gem—Citrine
Rules—Our mental function

The solar plexus is a most-powerful chakra. If someone is going to steal your energy, it's going to be here. I tell clients this is the area they need to protect at all times. I visualize a bright, yellow light encompassing my solar plexus, radiating inward and outward. Whenever you feel threatened or in danger, the solar plexus is the first chakra to alarm you. You'll feel a gnawing or anxious energy in the pit of your stomach. This is your powerhouse. The solar plexus is used to make things happen and to create power, so use it wisely. We feel all sorts of emotions at the solar plexus level. If we learn to channel these emotions into good things, prosperity and inner peace will occur. If we channel feelings negatively, egotism and arrogance can take over.

If this chakra is blocked, we feel repressed and think of ourselves as victims. The "pity parties" set in. Nothing seems to flow and everywhere we turn, our energy or efforts are thwarted. Blockage occurs when we deny our feelings or repress them. If you are angry, let it out in a healthy way. If you are upset in a relationship, don't shut your emotions off, because you will shut down.

As a relationship astrologer, I have seen many clients hurt and rejected by their partners. They shut their feelings off to avoid suffering. Little do they realize, they are hurting themselves more in the long run. Health problems manifest, such as a digestive tract blockage or migraine headaches. If your solar plexus is not functioning properly, you will experience stress, unstable sleep patterns, weight gain and perhaps depression.

However, you don't want your solar plexus to be open all of the time. If it is too open, it can be vulnerable to other people's energies. We are like a sponge and can "soak up" other's emotions and problems. All you need to do if you are around negative people or situations, is to envision a beautiful yellow light, like a ball of sunshine, surrounding and protecting your solar plexus area. This will help protect your personal power source.

When your solar plexus is open and secure, you can prosper in many ways. We have inner power to attain our goals and desires. We feel optimistic and energized!

The Heart Chakra

The heart chakra is the fourth chakra. This is the center for human love! It is located at the heart.

Color—Emerald green
Crystal/Gem—Rose quartz
Rules—The astral plane

The energy radiating from your heart chakra is a powerful healing energy. It can reach the one person you love or out into the entire universe. It depends on how you choose to direct it. I believe that love is the most powerful healer. The heart chakra gives us this special gift and, if used wisely, can affect our lives in more ways than imagined.

First, it can help us to accept and love ourselves. Second, it helps us to create, share, give and receive love from others. People who have difficulty with the heart chakra find it hard to love or even feel loved. Some problems lead to physical ailments such as heart conditions and high blood pressure. People with heart chakra blockages may not be able to forgive, or feel little compassion for their fellow man. While I have written of blocked chakras in previous pages, the heart chakra doesn't have to be closed or blocked for problems to arise. Leaving the heart chakra "too open", thus making people vulnerable to getting hurt, is also a major concern.

You will often see the heart chakra closed or blocked when

someone has gone through the loss of a loved one, such as a death, break-up, divorce or separation.

9/11 AND THE HEART CHAKRA

Many of us in the United States felt a block to our heart chakra, upon the attack of our country, on September 11, 2001, at the World Trade Center in New York. I myself went numb upon watching the tragic events unfold on television. Then a wonderful thing happened; many of us opened our heart chakras up again . . . to give love by joining together; praying, donating money or time to help victims and their families.

I visited Ground Zero on the 6-month anniversary of 9/11. We were taken up in groups aboard a platform for a 5-minute viewing of the area. No one said anything. There was nothing but silence. I can't speak for others there, but I felt numb. Then I started to feel angry. "How dare these terrorists do this to us!" When it was time to leave, I passed by memorials and photos of the victims taped to the side of a barricade. All of a sudden, something happened, I felt love . . . love for my country and our people. My heart chakra, once closed, in a matter of minutes was activated. By changing my thought pattern, I was able to open it again.

In extreme heart chakra blockages, people suffer from heart conditions and even heart attacks. It is often said that the inability to love can lead to a heart attack. A heart attack is, in essence, a broken heart.

A functioning and healthy heart chakra allows its owner to be creative, loving, accepting and happy with the world and at peace with oneself.

The Throat Chakra

The fifth chakra is our throat chakra. Its area is the throat. It can shut down when we don't communicate correctly, or hold things inside that need to be released.

Color—Blue
Crystal/Gem—Turquoise
Rules—The etheric body

When the throat chakra is up and running, we can speak our truths with self confidence and without hesitation. We listen well and do not judge others. What we have learned to feel in the solar plexus and heart chakra, we can verbally express through a healthy throat chakra. Without being able to communicate, our ability to share with others is greatly hampered. You've heard people refer to "a breakdown in communication". In such cases, it's likely someone's throat chakra is not working properly! Miscommunication between people is often a sign of this.

A blocked throat chakra can produce sore throats, tooth problems and swollen glands. Some feel an anxious energy and experience wild mood swings.

Many who suffer from a blocked throat chakra will come to find they aren't speaking up when they should. They suffer in silence. People are either afraid to speak up for fear of ridicule and rejection or just for wanting to keep peace. Others will use their voice to create lies and to manipulate others. This does major damage to the throat chakra. A lot of people avoid talking about an issue that is unpleasant, but at the same time, have a strong need to tell someone off. Now, opening the throat chakra doesn't mean you can go around telling everyone off. It *does* mean sharing our thoughts in a positive, spiritual manner.

A healthy chakra will give us the courage to speak up for our beliefs, to admit when we are wrong and listen to our inner wisdom.

The Brow Chakra

The sixth chakra is the brow chakra. It's located between our eyes. It provides us with gifts of insight, vision and wisdom.

Color—Indigo
Crystal/Gem—Quartz crystal
Rules—Celestial body

The brow chakra is not the psychic "third eye", although it is located between our other two. But it is the chakra of "seeing", not just in physical terms but in spiritual. Here, we can learn to use our intuition. The brow chakra helps us believe in magic!

When you reach your mid-20s, the brow chakra will probably start to develop and you'll recognize psychic powers. Sadly, some people never develop this chakra. Sometimes, the brow chakra develops in our 40s and 50s, after we have learned to trust the universe and all of its splendor.

I recall that at about age 25, my brow chakra started to grow, and by age 27, I was doing intuitive readings professionally.

If you can learn to strengthen this chakra, you can achieve not only great wisdom but also a sense of inner peace and "knowing".

People who need to work on their brow chakra will sometimes experience headaches, memory loss and nightmares. Some feel as if life has passed them by.

Those with a healthy brow chakra are excited about life. You'll be introduced to true power and spirituality. People gain an understanding that "whatever happens, happens for a reason".

Karmic relationships are drawn to you and easily recognized because you are open. You become the seeker of truth. With the development of this chakra, you gain much understanding.

Many healers and those in holistic and intuitive professions have highly developed brow chakras. These are the people who believe nothing will stop them from attaining their goals. They believe the universe will provide for them. This is not being naive. It is being open to extraordinary possibilities.

The Crown Chakra

Color—Purple
Stone—Amethyst
Rules—Highest spiritual plane

The crown chakra is the highest point in our energy field. It integrates the spiritual, intellectual, physical and emotional parts of us. This is the chakra that helps us connect to a higher source. Some people never develop this chakra in their lifetime. If and when it becomes developed, you will live your life based on love and peace. You will no longer crave the material possessions this world has to offer. You will devote your life to helping and teaching others on their spiritual path, much as Jesus did. You will be "enlightened" and very intuitive.

Balancing Your Chakras

I am going to teach you how to balance your chakras. Once you learn how to do this, you can complete the process very easily and quickly. If you're having a tough day or just feel out of balance, working on your chakras will help you to feel energized. Let's review a few points before we begin the process:

1. We have seven main chakra points in our body.
2. When we have emotional or physical pain, we shut our chakras down. We block ourselves sometimes:
   —By suppression of our feelings
   —Freezing or numbing our feelings
   —Depleting energy
   —Denying feelings
3. Here are a few things you can use as tools to help open or balance your chakras:
   —Gem stones coordinating to each chakra
   —Color fabric swatches coordinating with each chakra
   —A quiet place
   —Affirmations and visualization

When you balance the chakras, start from the bottom—at the root chakra—and work your way up. Some of your chakras may be working well. Others may be stuck or closed. You may need to spend only a few seconds in one area and perhaps a longer period in another.

I suggest you stand when you do these exercises. If you sit or lie down, the energy doesn't flow as easily.

THE ROOT CHAKRA

If the root chakra is not working, no other chakras will work. This is your gas tank.

1. Place your hand on the root chakra near the pelvic bone.
2. Close your eyes.

3. Visualize the color red vibrating in this area. Feel the warmth of the red encircling your root chakra.

4. Take a garnet stone and place it on the pelvic area. If you do not have a garnet, take a piece of red cloth or red paper and place it there.

5. Take a moment to feel the energy start to move in this area of your body. You may feel a tingling sensation or just a slight increase in energy. Some people will start to feel their body sway or rock back and forth. This means the root chakra is turned on and working! It may take as little as a few seconds or as much as a couple of minutes. Just be patient and visualize the color red.

6. Open your eyes and read the following affirmation:

I am grounded and free of fear. I release any blocks or negative energy immediately. I am open to receive the abundance of the universe!

THE SACRAL CHAKRA

1. Place your hand just below your belly button.
2. Close your eyes.
3. Visualize the color orange.
4. Place a carnelian stone or orange fabric on the belly button.
5. Feel the energy flowing in this area. Concentrate all of your energy on the sacral chakra.
6. Say the affirmation . . .

I experience wholeness with my masculine and feminine sides. Both are in harmony and balance. Serenity flows throughout me and within me.

THE SOLAR PLEXUS

1. Place your hand on your gut.
2. Close your eyes.
3. Visualize the color yellow in this area.
4. Hold a Citrine stone or yellow fabric swatch in this area.
5. Feel the energy moving within you.
6. Say the affirmation . . .

I have the power within me to create abundance, happiness and peace. I will reach my highest potential. I accept complete responsibility for my life.

THE HEART CHAKRA

1. Place your hand on your heart.
2. Close your eyes.
3. Visualize the color pink.
4. Place a green stone, an emerald or green color swatch on your heart.
5. Think of someone you love.
6. Concentrate on energy moving in this area.
7. Say the affirmation . . .

I am filled with the power of love. I love and accept my self. My heart is open to giving and receiving. I create and manifest love in my everyday life!

THE THROAT CHAKRA

1. Place your hand on your throat.
2. Close your eyes.
3. Visualize the color blue.
4. Place a turquoise stone or blue fabric against your throat.

5. Feel the energy move in your throat.

6. Say the affirmation . . .

I communicate through my head, my heart and my voice. I allow myself to express my thoughts, my desires and my feelings for my highest good and that of others.

THE BROW CHAKRA

1. Place your hand on your forehead.

2. Close your eyes.

3. Visualize the color indigo.

4. Place a quartz crystal or white fabric against your forehead.

5. Feel the energy there.

6. Say the affirmation . . .

I am complete. I am whole. My spirit, mind and body are at peace, working in harmony together. I am healthy. Radiant light shines within me, around me and through me.

THE CROWN CHAKRA

1. Place your hand on the top of your head.

2. Close your eyes.

3. Visualize the color purple.

4. Place an amethyst stone or purple fabric on top of your head.

5. Feel the energy move in this area.

6. Say the affirmation . . .

I accept all of the blessed things the universe brings to me for my highest good. My spirit is at peace. I am creating and enjoying a happy, healthy and prosperous life.

The Finishing Touch

To complete the chakra balancing process, you should take the time to "fluff" your aura and energy field. With your hands, make upward, swirling motions all over and around the body. This will help circulate and blend all of the positive energies and draw them upward.

HOW DO YOU FEEL?

You should feel relaxed but not tired. You should feel energized but not anxious.

Once you learn this process, you can go through the steps easily just by touching your chakra area and visualizing the colors as you work upward. Sometimes you'll notice that a particular chakra is constantly "blown" out. Picture a light bulb that's turned on and off and keeps blowing out. It happens to your chakras. How do you fix it?

Wear clothing of the specific colors that correspond to the chakra that needs more strength. If your heart chakra keeps blowing, wear a green shirt for a few days. Likewise you can wear the coordinating gemstones to enhance the energy of the chakras. You can also carry compatible crystals or wear a necklace designed with all seven stones. If you choose to wear loose stones, make sure they are somehow attached to your body. Carry a small pouch in your shirt pocket. If you get tired of wearing a particular color all of the time, you can always paint your toenails that hue! Women can wear bracelets and jewelry. If guys prefer not to wear jewelry, they can carry loose tumble stones in their pockets. These stones can be found in new age shops and at craft and gem shows for as little as 50 cents each.

There are other ways to cleanse the energy field of negativity and stress too. You can use Bach flower essences. Spray them in your auric field. Visualize a white light around your entire body. Practice relaxation techniques or meditate.

Earlier in the chapter, I discussed that it's not always good to leave your chakras open all the time, because they could accept people's negative energy. There are certain things you can do to shut down your chakras immediately if you need to.

CHAKRA PROTECTION

If your chakras are wide open and unprotected, it's easy to absorb another person's "junk". If we are in a room filled with people and someone is going through emotional pain, our chakras can zone in on that and actually take the pain on. Anger is easy to pick up. If you have a co worker or mate who is upset, you may feel their stress. Anger can really damage our chakras' vitality. Protecting and surrounding yourself with positive energy is like slipping into a coat of armor.

There are ways to balance and protect your energy field. You can use a white light meditation. It's probably the easiest and most simplest method to use. You can be anywhere and at anytime, just visualize a beautiful white light all around you. See it circling the entire body, from the top of your head to the tips of your fingers to the soles of your feet. Visualize this white light soaking into your body and giving you energy. When you are around anyone who is angry or anxious, just think of this white light all around you, protecting you from taking on their negative energies. We can soak in energy without even realizing it. We're like sponges, so it's important to protect ourselves with the white light. We can also offer healing to other people by visualizing white light around them even if they are not in our presence.

When I'm driving and see a car accident, I place a white light around the accident scene and the victims to send positive energy their way.

Because we are all affected by other people, emotionally, physically, mentally or spiritually, many of us need to balance our chakras every day. You can do it anytime you need to. The more you work with the chakras, the more natural the process becomes and you'll immediately know which chakra is not working properly.

The energy field is sacred. It is your power. If you use it correctly, take of it, and don't abuse it, you'll feel great and look good. Once you master this technique it is something you can do in a matter of minutes. You'll just place your hand on each energy point, visualize the color and feel the energy shift as you move from the root chakra to the top of the crown chakra.

NINE

*Crystals**

✦ ✦ ✦ In the past several years, "power bead" bracelets have become very popular. These are crystal or gemstone jewelry that attracts certain types of energy to it's wearer. In fact, you may own several pieces yourself. The idea behind the power bracelets is really not new. For thousands of years, people have been using crystals to help draw and create powers of healing, love, protection and prosperity.

---

*I have written about the use of crystals and gemstones in the chakra chapter. There are thousands more available to us than just the seven that were mentioned. The use of color and crystals is a big part of helping balance our energy, so it's only fitting that we look further into other uses as well.

Gemstones and crystals are part of nature, God's abundant creation. Crystals hold healing energies. These energies draw or vibrate to different things. One of the nicest crystals you can find for love and opening your heart chakra is the rose quartz. It is a soft pink color and helps heal broken hearts. It helps promote self-love too. If you're tired a lot, clear quartz crystal draws energy to you. It will give you that extra boost you need. Amethyst helps develop psychic abilities.

When you choose a stone or crystal, I suggest following your intuition. If a crystal warms up in your hand, it's energy will work with yours. If it remains cool to the touch, it's likely the energies of that particular stone are not responding to you.

For years I had a strong desire to find pink tourmaline jewelry. Not pink ice or garnet. Even the beautiful pink sapphires would not do. I was drawn to the pink tourmaline. It is not the easiest gemstone to find. So whenever I ran across a ring or necklace, I bought it. I felt something was missing if I didn't wear the stone or carry it with me. There are different colors of tourmaline, but the pink is a heart stone that strengthens wisdom and willpower. It enhances creativity too. The energies the stone had to offer were something I needed at that time in my life. I don't wear the tourmaline as much as I once did, but often find myself reaching for it at least once a week.

If there is something lacking in your life or perhaps some talent or virtue you'd like to strengthen, carry a stone that enhances it. You'll likely notice subtle differences after just a few days.

Here is another personal story I would like to share with you. About 10 years ago, I was going through a difficult separation in my relationship. I brought a rose quartz, heart-shaped pendant and wore it every day. I even slept with the necklace. Rose quartz, as mentioned earlier, helps heal broken hearts and draws love. I wore that stone for 9 months, until my ex came back into my life and wanted to work things out. The evening of our first date came and went; we had agreed to get back together. The next morning, I realized my rose quartz necklace was gone! It was nowhere to be found. I searched high and low for the thing. The clasp to the necklace was strong, so I knew it didn't break off. I came to the conclusion that the crystal had served its purpose and vanished. Its mission was completed. It played a part in bringing love back into my life. Other people have shared similar experiences they have had with their crystals vanishing in thin air.

Crystals can be used to create energy, to open up chakras, and to help with emotional balance. When you first buy a crystal, it is important that you cleanse it to make it yours. Since crystals absorb energy easily, you should release the energies of others who have touched it, before you use it. I always place my crystals in salt water over night. Never let anyone wear your crystals unless you want to carry their energy or issues around with you! Here's a simple guide to enhance your life through the power of crystals.

Crystal Guide

Agate—Carry this stone with you when taking a difficult exam or test. It will help keep you focused. If you're finding it hard to tell the truth, this stone will make it easier to 'fess up!

Alexandrite—If you're nervous about something, wear Alexandrite. It will calm you and take away the butterflies in your stomach.

Amazonite—This stone gets your creative juices flowing. If you have a bad habit you'd like to kick, Amazonite can help.

Amber—If you tend to be high strung and emotional, this stone will work wonders for you. It's known to heal and soothe, and brings harmony to its wearer.

Amethyst—This is February's birthstone, but anyone who wants to increase their psychic ability should use it.

Aquamarine—Reduces nervousness. If you frighten easily or have a fear of heights, this gem helps dissolve phobias.

Aventurine—Releases anxiety and fears. Wear it and you'll feel optimistic and happy!

Azurite—If you have a cold, carry this stone for a quick cure!

Bloodstone—If a shot of self confidence is what you need, carry the bloodstone around for a few days.

Barite—Your friendships and relationships will run more smoothly with this stone.

Blue Lace Agate—Soothes emotions and pain. It will help you relax.

Calcite (clear)—Helps overcome any fears you may have. By wearing this stone, you will know the difference between the truth and deception.

Calcite (green)—Releases fear. If you get stuck in a rut, the green calcite will help you come up with new ideas to reach your goal.

Calcite (pink)—Helps to let go of past hurts. Draws unconditional love to you.

Carnelian—Helps with grounding. You will feel more focused.

Celestite—If you are giving a speech or presentation before a group, wear this stone. It promotes creative expression.

Chrysocolla—Balances emotions. Reduces fear and anger. Helps upset stomach. Eases depression.

Citrine—Carry this stone to draw money or prosperity to you.

Diamond—Good healing stone. Intensifies the power of other stones.

Emerald—Works on all matters of the heart. When you're going through a break-up or just on the outs with your best friend, wear emerald to heal your heart.

Fluorite—Good for meditation. Strengthens teeth and bones. Hyper? This stone will calm you down.

Garnet—Inspires passion and love. Sleeping with it helps you remember your dreams.

Gem Silica—This is a rare and beautiful stone. Helps unlock the feminine side of a person's nature.

Hematite—If you get headaches, this stone could help relieve them.

Jade—Promotes universal love. Radiates divine, unconditional love Dispels negativity. Aids in dream study.

Jasper—Powerful healing stone.

Kansas Pop Rock—Need an energy boost? Grab a pop rock!

Kunzite—Used by many to kick addictions. Heals heartbreak. Enhances self-esteem and acceptance.

Kyanite—Helps with astral travel. Promotes truth, loyalty and reliability.

Lapis—Increases intuition and spiritual growth. A stone of royalty. Brings past emotional hurts to the surface for healing.

Lepidolite—If you have trouble sleeping, put this stone under your pillow. It will help you drift off easily.

Lodestone—Magnetic rock. Realigns chakras, energy and auric fields.

Moonstone—When there's trouble in your love life, the moonstone can help. It relieves frustrations and balances emotions.

Onyx—Relieves stress.

Opal—Absorbs negative energy and works with karma. Good for people who have eye trouble or wear glasses. Enhances intuition.

Pearl—Softens pains. Soothing, peaceful vibrations.

Peridot—Increases intuitiveness. Stimulates the mind, but reduces stress.

Pyrite—Gives you a more positive outlook on life.

Quartz—The "everything" crystal. Magnifies the intensity of other crystals. Keeps negative energy away. Good for meditation and communicating with spirit guides.

Rose Quartz—The love stone. Vibrates and draws love to you!

Rhodonite—Take this stone with you to class if you've been up all night studying. It improves memory. Dispels anxiety and confusion.

Ruby—Great love stone. Ruby promotes your zest and passion for life. It will help you fight off colds too.

Sapphire (Blue)—Gives psychic ability, creativity, loyalty and love. Helps with flow of spiritual energy.

Sapphire (Yellow)—Helps build creativity. Gives wearer strength and discipline. Good for working on creative ideas and projects.

Crystals

Smoky Quartz—Good for depression and fatigue. Enhances dream interpretation and channeling abilities.

Tiger Eye—Softens stubbornness. Helps one to see "both sides of the coin".

Topaz (Blue)—Promotes tranquility and peace. Soothing effect on the wearer. Gives creativity and self expression.

Tourmaline (Green)—This stone will make your brain work better!

Tourmaline (Pink)—Heart/love stone .

Tourmaline (Watermelon)—The best heart healer.

Tourmaline (Black)—Offers protection from negative people and enemies.

Turquoise—Good friendship stone. Give to someone you care about.

TEN

Candle Magic

*★ In the past several chapters, you've learned how color affects us. You've studied the auric field and learned to balance chakras. You discovered some personal uses for gems and crystals. Now, let's combine all of this newfound knowledge and put it to further use. We can combine color, crystals and gemstones with the act of candle burning, to create powerful energy. This energy can be directed to a single purpose or put out into the entire universe.

For centuries, people have been lighting candles while they pray for specific needs. Whenever anyone was sick in our family, my mother would light a green candle for healing. They'd feel better within hours. If she was short on money, mom would buy purple candles. She'd light them to send energy out into the universe as she said her novenas to St. Jude. Money would come from surprise sources over the next few days or she'd have a small winning on a lottery ticket. If there was turmoil in the family, she would light a white candle for peace and say her prayer to St. Joseph, the patron saint of families. To her, burning a candle meant giving her prayer or thought more spiritual energy.

Any time I travel, I enjoy visiting the old cathedrals and churches and lighting candles for special intentions there. One year, when I was going through a very difficult period, I made a pilgrimage to the St. Jude Shrine in Baltimore, Maryland, just to light candles and say prayers. St. Jude is the patron saint of hopeless cases. There are millions of devout followers all over the world. I was pleasantly surprised to find another St. Jude Shrine four blocks away from my home in New Orleans! When friends come to visit, we buy a sack of tea lights from the gift shop, light them in the grotto and pray for family and friends. There's even a peaceful meditation garden there.

Let's get back to the rules for candle burning. Buy a candle in a specific color for your need. Begin your prayer on the day of the week that's best suited to the intention.

Our family is Catholic, so we're used to saying 9-day novenas and we burn our candles for 9 days in a row for 1 hour each day. Many people who work with candles burn them for 7 days. Because this is the most-common practice, we will use this example.

To set up your candle rituals, you will need a nice, quiet area. You should burn your candles at the same time every day, in the same room and for the same intention. You should use a new candle each day. Place your candle in a clear crystal, metal, glass or wood holder and make sure it is secure. Do not leave it unattended at any time.

Place a crystal or gemstone that corresponds to the color and intention near the base of the candle. I suggest you burn the candle for 1 hour each day. If you cannot stay with the candle that long, burn it for at least 10 minutes each day.

As you light the candle, say your prayer or affirmation out loud. You can write your own affirmations or use the ones I've included.

Intentions & Affirmations

TO CREATE AND ATTRACT LOVE

Candle Color—Pink

Day—Begin your intention on Tuesday if you're a woman. A
man starts on Friday.

Crystal—Rose quartz

Affirmation: I draw divine love to me. I am filled with the power of love and attraction. I am open to receiving the love that is manifesting in my life.

TO REPAIR A BROKEN LOVE AFFAIR

Candle Color—Deep Purple

Day—Friday

Crystal—Rose quartz, pink tourmaline

Affirmation: Our relationship is healed and whole and
_____(put name here) and I are working on all of our issues for our highest good.

TO SAVE A MARRIAGE

Candle Color—Green

Day—Friday

Crystal—Rose quartz

Affirmation: I give thanks for the healing that is going on in my marriage. _____(put name of spouse here) and I are working together in peace, harmony and love for our highest good. Nothing can come between us and our love for one another.

TO MAKE NEW FRIENDS

Candle Color—Red

Day—Sunday

Crystal—Turquoise

Affirmation: The universe brings me new and true friends. I draw positive, kind and loving people to me.

TO STOP GOSSIP

Candle Color—Orange

Day—Monday

Crystal—Black tourmaline

Affirmation: My world is full of peace and harmony. There is no gossip, lying or manipulation around me. I will not allow negative thoughts or conversation near me.

TO PASS A TEST OR EXAM

Candle Color—Yellow

Day—Wednesday

Crystal—Carnelian

Affirmation: My mind is strong and clear. I am calm and relaxed as I take my test. I pass it with flying colors!

TO INCREASE YOUR PSYCHIC ABILITY

Candle Color—White

Day—Monday

Crystal—Amethyst

Affirmation: I am open to receiving all of the wonderful gifts the universe has to offer me. My intuitive abilities are strong and expanding.

FOR SELF CONFIDENCE

Candle Color—Red

Day—Sunday

Crystal—Bloodstone

Affirmation: I am confident, assured and wise. I know I can accomplish whatever it is I set out to do.

FOR PEACE IN THE FAMILY

Candle Color—White

Day—Thursday

Crystal—Jade

Affirmation: All is calm in our family. We are growing in love and light, peace and harmony each day. The white light of protection surrounds my family.

FOR A NEW JOB

Candle Color—Gold

Day—Sunday

Crystal—Citrine

Affirmation: I give thanks for the wonderful and fulfilling work that is coming my way. I am able to prosper and grow because of this new opportunity.

TO GET A PROMOTION

Candle Color—Red

Day—Sunday

Crystal—Citrine

Affirmation: I am ready to take the next step up at work. I am open and grateful for my new, expansive opportunity.

TO FIND FULFILLMENT IN EVERYDAY LIFE

Candle Color—Forest Green

Day—Friday

Crystal—Amber

Affirmation: My body, mind and spirit are at peace. I am excited, happy and thankful for all that I have. I look forward to each new day, fulfilling experiences and friends. I am grateful to be alive.

TO FIND INNER PEACE

Candle Color—Silver or white

Day—Monday

Crystal—Pearl

Affirmation: I am filled with joy and peace within. There is no reason for concern or worry. I am relaxed. My mind, body and spirit are calm.

FOR SAFE TRAVELS

Candle Color—Blue

Day—Thursday

Crystal—Quartz crystal

Affirmation: My travels are safe and happy, free of any delays or danger.

TO START A SUCCESSFUL DIET

Candle Color—Yellow

Day—Thursday

Crystal—Sodalite

Affirmation: I am losing weight in a healthy and relaxed manner. I am eating right and getting rid of all of my food addictions. I am able to control all of my cravings and maintain a good weight and healthy body image.

TO WIN A LAWSUIT

Candle Color—Blue

Day—Thursday

Crystal—Citrine

Affirmation: My legal issues are fulfilled in a positive, speedy and fair manner. I give thanks for the successful outcome.

TO MOVE

Candle Color—Orange

Day—Monday

Crystal—Quartz crystal

Affirmation: I am thankful for the new residential opportunities that are coming my way. I will find the perfect home, one that is affordable, beautiful and for my highest good.

TO SELL REAL ESTATE

Candle Color—Green

Day—Friday

Crystal—Emerald

Affirmation: My property is sold quickly and without any delays. I am pleased with the prosperity I have received from its sale.

TO GET RID OF NEGATIVITY

Candle Color—Black

Day—Saturday

Crystal—Black tourmaline

Affirmation: Any and all negativity has vanished. I am safe and protected by a positive environment, good people and my Guardian Angel. There is no room in my life for unpleasant people. I will not allow anything or anyone that is not of a pure intent to affect my life force.

TO GET PREGNANT

Candle Color—Light green

Day—Friday

Crystal—Quartz crystal

Affirmation: I give thanks for the opportunity to bear, love and raise a child. I am happily and easily becoming pregnant in a healthy and perfect manner.

TO MAKE A GOOD DECISION

Candle Color—Blue

Day—Thursday

Crystal—Green tourmaline

Affirmation: I give thanks for a clear mind. I am able to reach a solid decision for my highest good and that of others.

FOR LOVED ONES AT A DISTANCE

Candle Color—Orange

Day—Monday

Crystal—Quartz crystal

Affirmation: I give thanks for the protection of (put name here)_____. I am sending love and light to him/her across the miles.

FOR SOMEONE SICK

Candle Color—Green

Day—Anytime it is necessary

Crystal- Quartz crystal

Affirmation: (Put name here) _____'s health is improving immediately. He/she is full of strength, life and vigor. All sickness and disease is vanishing as I pray.

FOR SPIRITUAL GROWTH

Candle Color—Purple

Day—Thursday

Crystal—Amethyst

Affirmation: I am open to expanding my spirituality and, with it, the abundance the universe brings me.

TO WIN A CONTEST

Candle Color—Green

Day—Friday

Crystal—Citrine

Affirmation: I am lucky and fortunate. Good things come my way.

ELEVEN

Numerology

Your Birth Number Reveals All!

Is the day you were born considered lucky or cursed? Do the numbers in your birth date add up to success? Numerology, the study of numbers, can shed some light on your personality traits and life path.

Numbers have power. Your favorite sports team chants, "We're Number One!" Seven is considered lucky. Unlucky 13 is to be avoided. Heaven forbid if the 13th falls on a Friday! Over the course of history and for thousands of years, the ancient science of numerology has been taught, researched and taken seriously by many. In modern times, numerology is used more as a new age tool.

IF YOU CAN ADD,
YOU CAN LEARN NUMEROLOGY, TOO.

We can trace the origins of numerology back to the Greek mathematicians and philosophers from sixth-century BC. According to their studies, each number has a personality of its own. Odd numbers have stronger energy than even numbers and a more powerful vibration. They are regarded as masculine. Even numbers carry less strength and are said to be feminine. Why are odd numbers stronger? Because when you add odd numbers to even, the result is always an odd number.

Mystics and philosophers also believed that the human psyche is already determined at birth and can be divided into nine stereotypes of the primary numbers, one to nine. This is where the basic birth number system many numerologists use today came from. The formula is easy to learn. You'll be amazed at how accurate it is.

HOW TO DETERMINE YOUR BIRTH NUMBER:

The process is simple. Write out the day, month and year in which you were born. For example if you were born on October 12, 1985, you would write down the number like this:

10/12/1985

Then add together the numbers in three separate parts (month, date, and year).

Example: **Month** 1+0= 1   **Day** 1+2 = 3   **Year** 1+9+8=5= 23

Now add the three totals together: 1+3+23 = 27
Reduce the final number to a single digit of 9 or less:

27 is 2+7=9

The birth number for someone born on October 12, 1985, is the number 9.

To Find Your Birth Number

Write down your *birthday* _____
Write down your *month* of birth _____
Write down your *day* of birth _____
Write down your *year* of birth _____

This paragraph is important! There are two numbers that are very special numbers. They are called *master numbers* and are explained in the last part of this chapter. If your final number adds up to 11 or 22, do not reduce it to a single digit. These are the only two numbers you do not reduce. People born with these birth numbers have special purposes that will be explained later.

Birth Numbers

NUMBER ONE

Number One people are leaders. They are independent, fiery and have great organizational abilities. They usually have strong minds. They are not always at the top of their game, but gifted in some way. Number Ones need to be the "best" at something. They are competitive and expect to win. They want to be noticed, adored and loved.

In younger years, Number Ones enjoy hanging out with adults rather than kids their own age. They are more mature than most of their peers. Some are known to marry fairly young and have troubled relationships. It's best for Number Ones to wait until they're older to settle down. They can be self-centered and overachievers, leaving little time and attention for their mates.

They think they can "have it all", and will do their best to get ahead in life. Many times they do. If you are a Number One, consider yourself lucky; you'll have a lot of enthusiasm for life and won't take "no" for an answer. You surely won't settle for being Number Two! In your heart, you know you are special. You recognize that you deserve great things, and work hard to make them happen. Just don't be too critical and impatient with others who may not see things your way.

The nice thing about Number Ones is that they have a great ability to take charge and get things done. If a co-worker is having trouble with the boss, you'll offer sound solutions. If a committee needs a chairperson, you're up for the job. You have a lot of confidence and energy. Why shouldn't people believe in you? Everyone looks to you for leadership. That's why many Ones are popular or respected on the job. They don't wait for things to happen. They *make* things happen! One of the biggest differences between you and most other folks is that you are an "achiever". You will let nothing stand in your way. Some people may call you ruthless, cocky and even arrogant. Take it as a compliment. Don't let them bother you. You know you have what it takes to succeed! Go after your dreams!

Famous Number Ones include George Washington and Martin Luther King, Jr.

NUMBER TWO

If you're a Number Two, compassionate, caring and loving would best describe you. Twos draw many people into their lives who teach them lessons about love. They benefit when working in partnerships and groups. These folks are not overly aggressive. They strive for peace and harmony.

Since Twos are here to work on "affairs of the heart" and getting along with others, close ties are important. Friendships, family and other loved ones will be major players in a Two's life. Many of these relationships have a fated quality about them; perhaps dealing with past life issues and karma.

A few Twos find relationships troubling; either they can't meet the "right one" or they have a problem with settling down, even though they desperately want to. This is all part of the lesson they are here to learn. Not only do Twos need other people but they need to learn about the mechanics of relationships; what it takes to make love work, along with compromise and balance.

Romance is so important for Twos. Women often plan their wedding day years before it happens. Men long to be the knight in shining armor for their queens. Both sexes usually believe in the theory of soul mates.

If a Two is dateless or single for long, they feel empty. It's really important for them to be in a stable, secure relationship. Sometimes, their love life takes precedent over a career and other relationships in their lives. Once in a committed affair, Twos settle in nicely and are joined at the hip with the object of their affections.

Because Twos get so caught up in love, they can neglect their friends. This is an area they need to work on. If your friend is a Two and currently single, don't count on things staying the same in your relationship, when they fall in love. They really don't mean to ignore you, it's just that love consumes them.

But when there's a break-up, guess whose shoulder they'll cry on? If you are a Two, it's important to keep a balance in your everyday life, between all of your relationships: friends *and* lovers.

Love is grand, but don't miss out on all of the other wonderful things life has to offer.

Famous Number Twos include Bill Clinton, Madonna and Prince Charles.

NUMBER THREE

Threes are communicators. They are creative and imaginative. Many make excellent teachers, writers and artists. Some are quick-witted and have a good sense of humor. Their masterminds are constantly ticking. Higher education and learning new things excite Threes. Most are open to trying new things; however, some Threes can be very cautious. It's important that they don't allow fear or phobias to deny them experiences that may enrich their lives. Ride the roller coaster at least once!

The Three places a big emphasis on friendship. They enjoy going out in groups. The social scene is important and they love just hanging out. Travel is a big deal too. Bribe them with a trip to Hawaii and they'll do anything!

Some Threes are known for their elaborate collections—from antiques to tea cups to race car models. Their collections are usually valuable and they keep them for years, hating to part with memorabilia, mostly because of sentimental value.

Those born with this birth number can be a little fickle in love. They like variety and change, but once they make a commitment, it's usually solid. Threes want a lover who will really listen to them. They want someone with whom they can share their deepest feelings. It's important they are listened to and taken seriously in a relationship.

With a natural-born gift of gab, Threes can burn up the phone lines! They enjoy good gossip and are known to be blabbermouths! Don't tell a Three your darkest secret unless you want it broadcast all over town! (Just kidding.)

Threes are good-hearted people. They usually keep friends for life, all the way from kindergarten to old age. They'll remember your birthday every year!

If you're a Three, you should make sure to use all of your God-given creative talents. We all are born with a special gift. It is our responsibility to the universe to use these gifts to help others in some way. Threes are blessed with a variety of talents: creativity, musical ability, communication skills and teaching capabilities. So, if you have a beautiful voice, make music with it. If you can write, become a reporter or novelist. If you excel in a certain subject, teach others. By helping society, your talent will grow! If you don't use it, you'll lose it. Giving of yourself and helping others along their spiritual path is why we're all on planet earth anyway!

Famous Number Threes include Bill Cosby and F. Scott Fitzgerald.

NUMBER FOUR

If you're a Number Four, you are dependable and trustworthy. You are nurturing and sympathetic. Fours like to help others, but need to be appreciated for their efforts. Family ties are very important. You are likely to be close to your mother. Fours are serious-minded and prone to work in a service-oriented industry. Some Fours need an extra push to go out into the world. They want to succeed and often do, but *Home Sweet Home* is hard to leave. They are most happy, once they have a spouse and children of their own. Yes, they can be homebodies, but if given the right kind of encouragement, Fours can be dynamite in the corporate world too.

These are "salt-of-the-earth" people. If you're a Four, people know they can depend on you. You will hate to be late for anything. You're also the thoughtful one who seldom forgets a best friend's birthday, your parent's anniversary or to call Aunt Bea every Sunday. Family heirlooms, genealogy and children are things you hold dear. A sense of belonging to something is important, whether it be the school PTA or community council. Sharing with others and working together makes you feel happy and secure.

You're probably good with little kids. You may have a special connection with your pets. You sense people's pain and feel empathy for others. Because of these nurturing qualities, Fours make great doctors, nurses, counselors and teachers.

Fours need to feel that they fit in and "belong". They try hard to please people. They want everyone to like them, so they may go overboard to win approval. Some are perfectionists.

In relationships, they like to date one person at a time, and a relationship can last for years. Some marry their childhood sweethearts.

Fours' lesson is to take more risks and try new things. If you don't accept change, or if you hang on too tightly to the past, you could get stuck in a rut and life will become boring.

Your life is what you make it, filled with challenges, opportunities and new experiences. Think "out-of-the-box" once in a while and you'll be pleasantly surprised!

Famous Number Fours include Arnold Schwarzenegger and Demi Moore.

NUMBER FIVE

Fives are creative and love change. They are here to conquer the world and usually have many goals they want to accomplish. Some are into music, art and creative writing. Their minds are strong and some have high IQs. They just don't like to sit long enough to prove it! Sometimes, Fives enjoy the chase more than the conquest. They love working towards a goal rather than reaching it.

In love, they can date more than one person at a time and enjoy playing the field. Flirting is a favorite pastime and they master the art like no other! Fives don't always need to be in a relationship. They feel comfortable in their own company and are known to go without a steady relationship for years. These folks are hard to tie down for long! Some have been known to be foot-loose and fancy-free well into their late forties.

Change is important to them. If their life is too steady or com-placent, they'll stir the pot a little and cause a bit of a ruckus, just to keep the party going! And speaking of parties, Fives throw the best bashes. Because they are spontaneous, anything can happen. Fives always seem to land on their feet. In sticky situations, they come out smelling like a rose. The punishment doesn't always fit the crime. They get away with a lot.

Fives win popularity contests. Seldom do people say bad things about them, except for their jilted lovers! Lucky in love, they could break a few hearts along the way. Fives don't mean to hurt anyone, they just look at life as one big party. Therefore, Fives may not always stick to a specific game plan in life. There are too many choices.

You may find them changing their college majors more than once. They'll work a lot of odd jobs, never staying too long in any place. Fives are the type of people who make millions with their own inventions or happen to fall luckily into something. They are at the right place at the right time.

Experiences are what life is about. "Live life to its fullest". "You only go around once". "Make the most of every day". These are some of the mottoes Fives live by!

Famous Number Fives include Mick Jagger and Abraham Lincoln.

NUMBER SIX

If you're a Number Six, you may prefer a structured and disci-plined life. You are apt to be concise, intellectual and a deep thinker. Most Sixes have their lives planned out at about age seven or so. They know what they want to do when they get older or have a good idea of what they don't want to do! Many start careers early on and are good, honest, dependable workers.

Sixes have their share of luck and *then* some. They can attain great wealth if they work hard at it. They enjoy the finer things that life has to offer. Sometimes that means status symbols: expensive sports cars and designer clothes. Most of these people are attractive and charismatic. Often they are found taking on leaderships roles. People look up to them. If they're not careful, they run the risk of an inflated ego—but Sixes are mostly down to earth.

You will find many success stories among Sixes. In younger years, these kids were known to be "teacher's pet", winning awards and playing on the all-star team. In later years, Sixes have their share of trophies too. They seem to be able to fit a great deal into their lives: work, a family, a volunteer group and maybe a college course or two. Their lives are always full of things to do, and Sixes wouldn't have it any other way. Sixes are the super Moms and corporate fathers who squeeze anything and everything in to an 18-hour day.

Success is usually theirs, because they work hard for it. Sixes have priorities. Most of the time, working their way up the career ladder is at the top of their list, followed by family and then a social life.

In relationships, Sixes are not mushy romantics. They are polite, reserved and respectful. Appearances matter. They feel the person they date is a reflection of themselves. Often they will only date the nice-looking, the educated or people they feel have "potential". Indeed, they are picky! What others think of them matters, but not nearly as much as Sixes think of themselves.

Famous Number Sixes include Steven Spielberg and Stevie Wonder.

NUMBER SEVEN

The positive traits of the Number Seven are compassion and generosity. As a small child you were probably kind to all of your playmates. If someone was hurt, you tried to comfort them. Sevens are also very witty. They have a great sense of humor and know exactly what to say to make everyone smile!

You can be very romantic and a make a delightful partner. Sevens have their share of affairs and admirers. They are honest with their feelings, but do not like to fight or argue. Sometimes they will avoid confrontations, but when a love affair turns sour, they can walk away.

Although Sevens are not usually at the top of their class or promoted to a CEO position, they are smart. They daydream a lot. Reading is a favorite pastime. Movies and music too.

Many Sevens find new age and the occult interesting, because they tend to look at the world from a spiritual perspective. They're always searching for answers. When Sevens were younger, they pestered their parents for answers. They were always asking, "Why?", out of curiosity about the mysteries of life. Years later, Sevens are still searching, but have either developed faith or skepticism in the world around them. Some Sevens are very psychic individuals. They're born with a "sixth sense", and if nurtured and developed, can use their intuitive powers to get ahead in life.

Sevens are fascinating people. They are interesting to talk to and have many friends of different ages and backgrounds. They make good counselors, business people, ministers, politicians, lawyers and negotiators. A positive attitude is one of their greatest attributes. They believe in equality, fairness and social justice. So, many are drawn to humanitarian causes. They'll work hard to improve conditions in their own backyard, community or society as a whole. Sevens want to help make the world a better place in which to live. Many can and do make a difference.

Famous Number Sevens include John F. Kennedy and Princess Diana.

NUMBER EIGHT

Consider yourself lucky if you're an Eight. Eights draw money to themselves easily. You're one hard worker who'll get a raise without having to ask for it. Or you'll be born into money. If not, you may marry into it! Financial opportunities and stock tips could drop at your feet. There may be an inheritance in your future too. Some Eights are spoiled. If they are not well-off, Eights will treat themselves as if they were. They make sure their children have the little extras only money can buy.

As Eights mature, they want to make their own money and are determined to go after a good job that pays well. Many become affluent and quite successful. However, they should learn not to take everything so seriously. Money isn't everything. Often it's the Eight who works overtime on Sunday and holidays, forgoing family activities because there's money to be made. Take the time to relax and enjoy life. The bills will still be there. Work will be there. There's plenty of time for all of that. Remember to enjoy other the things that life has to offer.

Eights are always coming up with ways to make another buck or convince someone to invest in their latest idea. Some people call you a hustler. Others will say you're aggressive and a go-getter. You know that one day you'll be rich!

Status symbols and nice clothes are important. Designer labels are a must. Even though you're not always into the latest fads, "fitting in" is important. Keeping up with the Jones' could be very important. It's not that Eights are all materialistic. They want money to enjoy life, to be able to afford experiences like traveling to Europe in the summer, going to the latest movies, having a nice music system and of course, treating friends every now and then. Eights are generous people and enjoy giving as much as they do receiving.

When it comes to affairs of the heart, Eights can be just as generous. Buying cute cards and little presents for their honey, gives them much delight. When they fall in love, they fall hard and fast. They'll do whatever it takes to make a relationship work. Their hearts are sometimes even bigger then their wallets!

Eight's lesson is to learn to enjoy the true luxuries of life—people, home, family and love.

Famous Number Eights include Barbara Streisand and Elizabeth Taylor.

NUMBER NINE

Number Nine is the most powerful number of all because it contains the qualities of all numbers. Nine stands for energy, and most nines are full of life and vitality. They don't plan and plot a lot, they just act! They are strong-willed people who do not bend easily. Nines are restless souls and quite impulsive. They have quick tempers. Most of the time they are cheerful and optimistic.

As little kids, they can be "monsters", but lovable ones. Nines seem to get their way all of the time. That's because they never give in. Nines are accused of being spoiled brats. It's not their fault! In their defense, the adults in their life made them so! They allowed them to get away with things. It's hard to say, "No!", to their angelic faces and sweet pouts, even as they age!

Nines usually do well in the game of life. Academics aren't

their strong point, so you'll find them using their talents to shine in other ways. Most want to cut Mom's apron strings and leave home sooner than their siblings. They want to backpack cross country, move to another state or conquer the world! It's important for Nines to complete their education. Their lust to see the world could deter them. This is not a good thing. Sometimes they don't go back to school. Their lives take a lot of twists and turns. Other things become priorities.

If they marry young, before age 25, the union may end in divorce court. Nines should wait until their late 20s or early 30s to settle own. A relationship has more staying power by then. Their wanderlust is tamed and Nine is ready to make a permanent commitment.

It is so important in the early years that Nines stay on a specific path or have a disciplined agenda. Otherwise, they could set themselves up for failure and it could take years to get back on track.

Nines should make a plan and stay on course with it. Don't give up if the going gets tough. Most Nines can conquer the world if they set out to do so, but it needs to be done in an orderly fashion to avoid unnecessary crisis.

Famous Number Nines include Shirley MacLaine and Mahatma Gandhi.

NUMBER ELEVEN

If your birth number reduces to eleven, then *don't further reduce it to two*. Eleven is a special number, in a special category outside the basic numerology system that covers numbers one to nine. Eleven is a master number. Number Elevens people are considered to be higher, spiritual beings. If you fall into this category, you have great psychic powers.

You can rise to the top in your chosen profession. There is no gray area for the Number Eleven. You are either very positive or very negative when it comes to your way of thinking.

The positive Elevens achieve great things. The negative ones drift through life. The appear cool and aloof. If you're an Eleven, you are blessed with special powers. Use them for your highest good. Don't waste the potential you have within you to accomplish great things!

You dream big and those wishes can come true. The power of your mind is very strong. If you believe something will happen, it does. Say, you want to own a business one day. You can easily imagine how your office is laid out. You visualize every little detail. You know in your heart that you will be successful. There is no doubt! Things manifest for you. They just happen, if you believe. It's almost effortless!

Love is the same way. Once you set your sights on that special someone, you have eyes for no one else. You can draw that person to you. Elevens mesmerize people. So, you have these wonderful spiritual gifts; intuitive powers, the ability to manifest great things and powerful attraction. What do you do with them? These are presents from the universe. Open them, use them correctly and for your highest good. If you work from your heart, out of an unselfish and giving attitude, the entire world opens up to you. Seize your inner power, channel it correctly and make all of your dreams come true!

Famous Number Elevens include Jackie Onassis and Shirley Temple.

NUMBER TWENTY-TWO

Twenty-Twos are unique and special individuals. Number Twenty-Two is the number of the truly exceptional person. If the

qualities of the Twenty-Two are developed, they combine all of
the best influences from the other numbers, and one can achieve
greatness. Twenty-Two possesses the following strength or character from each of the numbers used in the system.

#1—Intelligence
#2—Sensitivity
#3—Energetic
#4—Ethical and hard-working
#5—Ambitious
#6—Charisma
#7—Psychic vision
#8—Determination
#9—Courage
#11—Idealism

If not spiritually developed, Twenty-Twos can be dreamers and
schemers. Some are workaholics and prone to arrogance. But if
Twenty-Two people use their abilities, they can go very far in life.
The true purpose of life should be service to others. Because you
have such a vast array of abilities, you should share your talents
and resources with others. Do you know someone special? Do you
say to yourself, "That guy has it all."? Charisma, luck, success. He
could be a Number Twenty-Two, who is using the magic of his
birth number correctly.

If you're a Twenty-Two, please recognize that you have great
power within you. You have been placed on this planet to do extraordinary things with this power. Yes, you could be president of
the country. You could develop a world peace plan. *You* can make
a difference in the world. Don't ever give up on a wish or desire. If
it is for your highest good, it will happen. You just need to learn to
have more patience. This is the lifetime in which you can attain

goals that most people would consider out-of-reach. Don't let negative people say you can't accomplish something. If you believe it, you can achieve it. You are blessed. Please don't waste this lifetime. It would be a crime to do so!

Famous Number Twenty-Twos include Kirk Douglas and Ann Bancroft.

TWELVE

Maria Shaw's Predictive Numerology

★ ★ ★ You've discovered your birth number and the personality traits associated with it. Now let's look at predictive numerology. I've designed my own numerology formula to help you predict the next 9 years of your life. This is a simple formula that's easy to learn. I've used this method for thousands of clients over the past 10 years, and it has never failed. In this numerology formula, our lives run in 9-year cycles. Each cycle has a different meaning. We deal with different issues and emphasis is placed on a certain path in our life each year. The cycles run birthday-to-birthday, rather than calendar-year-to-calendar-year.

HERE'S THE FORMULA
YOU'LL NEED TO DISCOVER YOUR

Numerology Number for the Year:

First Step: Take your birth month and add it to your day of birth. (Do **not** include the year.)

Example: June 4th = 6 + 4 = 10

This is the tricky part: You add the above number to the Current Year Master Number. These follow.

Year	Master Number
2002	40
2003	41
2004	42
2005	43
2008	44
2009	45
2010	46
2011	47

So for a June 4th birthday in 2002, you add 10 and 40 (the master number for the current year) and get 50.

Take that last number and reduce it to it's lowest single digit:

50 = 5+0 = 5

There you have your number for the year. In the example, it's the number 5.

It is extremely important to remember that this numerology does not run calendar-year-to-calendar-year. It runs from your birthday to your next birthday. For example, if your next birthday falls on

December 31, 2003, you cannot use the Master Year Number for 2003 until you reach your birthday. You will still be working with 2002's Master Year Number until the end of 2003. If your birthday is April 1, 2003, you will be working with the 2002 Master Year Number for the first 4 months of the calendar year. Then, in April, you begin using the 2003 Master Number.

Numerology Cycles

NUMBER ONE YEAR

This is a year of bright, beautiful beginnings. The emphasis is on **you**! Your needs, wishes and dreams will be the focus. I always tell clients that when you're in a Number One Year, you can get *anything* you want, but you need to ask for it. No one is going to hand you anything on a silver platter. You may have to ask more than once for your heart's desire, but it's likely you'll receive it.

Anyone coming into a Number One Year should take the time to make up a wish list. This is most effective when done on your birthday. The list should include everything you want; big and small. It doesn't matter if some of the things sound silly. Just write them down. This is *your* year. Your list can include more money, a new love, a better job, a scholarship, a dream car or inner peace. I recall a friend of my mine, who put "marriage" at the top of her list on her June birthday. By October, she was walking down the aisle in Las Vegas! I made up my wish list and 13 out of the 14 wishes came true over the course of the 12 months.

The thing to remember when you make your list, is to be very specific. You could write, "I want to date more this year", but then every jerk in town may ask you out! But if you were to write, "I want to meet a nice, attractive mate", chances are you'll be happier with what the universe brings you! Write, "I want a job that

I'll enjoy and that pays $25 an hour", rather than "I want a new job". The more details, the better!

Number One years are good for landing a new position in which you'll take on more responsibility and learn new skills. The new friends that enter your life now will be beneficial in some way. If you're starting a new project or moving, expect things to go well. Number One years are for all types of new beginnings and they can influence how the next 9 years of your life pan out. So make the most of this time.

NUMBER TWO YEAR

Are you looking for love? This is a good year to find it! Your Number Two Year is a period in which new relationships waltz into your life, romance blossoms and you are ready to fall madly in love! If all of your friends are dating, you'll want to find a special someone too. If you're single this year, you may be a little depressed if your dance card is not filling up. Therefore, one should be more aggressive in romance. This is the time to take the chance and ask someone out. You'll be pleasantly surprised. If friends want to fix you up on a blind date, it may not be a bad idea. Go ahead and accept. Love could be right around the corner.

If you are in a steady relationship, a deeper commitment is made. This is usually not considered a marriage year in numerology, rather a time to grow closer together. Engagements are announced, or you could decide to purchase joint property. Love Problems? You'll work through them easily now.

Even your friendships flow more smoothly this year. Love seems to be flowing through everyone you meet. It's a time when many people discover true love!

By the time the Number Two Year is in full swing, most people are happy with their love life. If you're not, it may be time to think about breaking new ground. Get out and travel in new circles, meet new people, make new friends. This year, anything can happen in love. Be sure to always look your best when you go out, because you never know who you'll meet. A real hottie could be eyeing you at the laundromat or in the grocery aisle!

The Number Two Year is favorable for partnerships of any kind, including business. If you're thinking of joining a venture with a pal or reputable associate, the union will prove to be rewarding. Likewise, if you're working with someone on an important project for an employer, the effort will be appreciated and will run smoothly!

Remember this is a "Two-to-Tango" year. You can double your pleasure in more ways than one!

NUMBER THREE YEAR

Communication, travel and creative pursuits fill this cycle. You won't feel much like getting down to business. Your popularity is on the rise now and you'll be attending lots of parties and special events.

New and long-lasting friendships could develop. Any clubs or organizations you join, will be beneficial. Let the good times roll! This is a year to hang out with the crowd and enjoy life. Have all the fun you can handle now, because when your Number Four Year rolls around, there won't be time.

Your social life is in full-swing and frankly that's all you care about this year. There are plenty of party invitations. Your day-planner will be filled. It'll be hard to find you home much. You're on the run all the time and you could get a new car too.

Your personal spending habits may get out of control as you find yourself shopping more. Music, CD players, new television sets and a personal computer are "must haves". You could get a cell phone too. Set limits. Don't let the talk time get out of hand. Long distance bills could be higher than you ever imagined!

Friends will make huge demands on your time. You may have to prioritize, to get work done on schedule. You'll be tempted to let responsibilities go now and then. Not a good idea—you could fall behind in regular tasks and duties because of your increased social activities.

Any type of group involvement, whether it be social or work-related is favorable. The contacts you make now could prove to be valuable in the coming years. Make an effort to shake hands with everyone!

This is also a year in which you'll take a dream vacation! Don't stay home and feed the cats. Register for frequent-flyer miles and buy new luggage. You'll be glad you did, because there's much travel in store. Sports and hobbies will expand. Your personal interests shine too. This is your "fun" year. Enjoy it, but keep a balance in your life at the same time.

NUMBER FOUR YEAR

This is the best year to get a promotion, evaluation or even a new job. You can increase your income too. If you do, it will be through your own hard work.

Your social life takes a back seat. Often your love life will be dull or you'll be too busy working to notice. You won't have as much time to spend with friends. Most people land a new position, but work hard trying to balance it with family and other responsibilities. You'll be thinking about serious issues, such as your 401K plan and career advancements.

Much can be gained if you work hard. You'll feel good about the doors that are opening for you and be more serious about specific goals. Using your time wisely is a must. This is a year in which you will feel successful, as if your hard work is paying off. If you've been working diligently, superiors will notice. Some people opt to change careers in the Number Four Year or go back to school. Whatever you are doing, it will seem as if there's more recognition and reward for your time and effort.

Opportunities may drop into your lap. You could be given an amazing position. Your boss will offer praise more than ever before. There will be times when you'll have to choose between work and play, between hanging out with your friends and clocking in on a Saturday night. Work will likely win out.

In fact, it will seem as if all you do is work. You'll beat a path from home to the office to the grocery store, home and then back to work again. Know that your hard work is not in vain. You are gaining ground. You are getting ahead. Things will slow down a little and there will be more time to relax when your Number Five Year rolls around. For now, you will make more money than ever before.

Promotions are likely. Ask for a raise at work; you'll get it. The interesting thing about a Number Four Year is that you really *want* to work. You look forward to it. If there's a job you've had your eye on, this is the year to apply. Many people get big breaks now, gain valuable contacts and experience a lot of luck during their Number Four cycle.

NUMBER FIVE YEAR

This is the year to fall madly in love! This is also a time of many romantic options. It seems as if everyone is interested in you. You may have your eye on more than one person, too! Know that you'll attract some wonderful people; unfortunately, you'll draw your share of losers too!

A Number Five Year can coincide with meeting your soul

mate. The lover you meet this year will be one you won't ever forget. You may easily hang onto the memory of this special person for years. Because it is also a romantic time, you could get lost in a fantasy world or caught up in day dreams. This is not a major commitment year but the mate you meet now could lead to a deeper promise or marriage, if you're still together 2 years from now.

You'll love all the attention and want to date as much as you can. Hormones are raging too and, if you're sexually active, you run the risk of a pregnancy this year. Take precautionary measures or abstain if you want to avoid this aspect.

A lot of people move to a new residence during a Number Five Year cycle. Just as many find they are remodeling the house or buying a vacation home somewhere. Five is a year of change and it's mostly good. You may want to re-do everything!

You'll want to update your personal look too. Changes in hairstyles, new clothes and a new attitude emerge. You're redefining who you are with the way you look and dress.

There will be many changes this year regarding your likes and dislikes. If you've always loved vanilla ice-cream, now you are ordering rocky road. Your tastes in fashion and friends are changing too. It's a bittersweet year . . . letting the past go, crossing the bridge from yesterday to tomorrow, but change is good!

NUMBER SIX YEAR

The Number Six cycle is a year in which you have a strong desire to get your life in order. If you're not happy with life, you'll work to improve your situation. If you hate your job, you'll send out resumes. If friendships become stale or boring, you'll look elsewhere for fun.

This is a good time to break bad habits. You can stop smoking, drinking or biting your nails now. Your taxes will be filed on time.

Organization is this year's buzz word. During Six Year, you get rid of what's not working for you and replace it with something that will. You'll toss out old paperwork and clothes collecting dust in the attic closet. You'll pitch Christmas cards from holidays past and all of the shoes you bought but never wore. You hate clutter now. Mother would be pleased!

If there is something you wish to accomplish, one can succeed. It's a great time to lose weight, get in shape or undergo intense physical training. If you set your mind to do something, determination and willpower will see you though. The power of the mind is very strong and there is little at which you can't succeed.

Some people say the Number Six Year is boring. Nothing exciting happens. This is somewhat true. I remember when I was going through my Six cycle, I inherited my parent's home and was responsible for the cleaning and selling of over 30 years of accumulation. It was not an easy task. I had estate sales for two weekends in a row. I was then in the mood to organize my own house and had another huge rummage sale. I got rid of a lot of stuff and extra clutter. It's piling up again but I know that when my Six Year rolls around, I'll have another sale!

Six is not about excitement and fun. It's about organization, duty and responsibility. So, if you're waiting to get your life in order and clean up your act, the Number Six Year calls on you to do this. It will help you accomplish much if you truly want to.

NUMBER SEVEN YEAR

This is what I call your "legal" year. You could merely be fighting a traffic ticket or engaged in a major lawsuit. Know that you are likely to win your case or, at least, the outcome will be fair and better than expected.

Anything your name is on looks good too. So, put out those

resumes for a new job and ask for a raise by putting your request in writing. You may even see your picture in the newspaper. The Seven Year is a time of recognition. You will stand out in a crowd. People notice you and acknowledge your accomplishments. Go ahead—toot your own horn!

If you're taking college courses, grades should be improving this year and the opportunities that arise can be most advantageous. You may make the Dean's List at school or be employee-of-the-month at work. If you have to prepare a speech or give a presentation of any kind, it will go over well. Interviews, auditions and applications are all part of this cycle. Apply for loans and scholarships too.

You may also be lucky. Entering drawings and raffles is a good idea. If you are job hunting, it's important that you write a personal letter with your resume. Superiors will appreciate the extra effort. Some younger adults may sign with the army or navy at this time.

Seven is a very spiritual number, so this year will be filled with higher thinking on your part. You may become enlightened about a spiritual path or have a strong desire to study occult matters. Many people connect with their spirit guides or guardian angel now. You may have a strong desire to study different religions. People you meet will likely have a profound effect on your life at this time. New mentors could appear. You'll be feeling more intuitive during this period and will likely expand your own psychic abilities.

Because this is a legal year, many marriages and divorces occur. If you met a soul mate in your Number Five Year, there could be wedding bells now. If a marriage has turned sour and you've been contemplating ending it, this is the time you'll likely call an attorney.

NUMBER EIGHT YEAR

You could hit the jackpot this year! This is an excellent money period. The Eight Year brings money to you effortlessly. Financial rewards do not always have to come via your job. Expensive gifts, clothes and trips could come your way. Since you'll have more money at your disposal, you can invest in hobbies and other interests.

This is a great time to ask for a raise at work. Everywhere you go, you'll run into good deals, sales and money opportunities. Some people start a serious savings plan. Whether you stash some cash in your dresser drawer or open an account with your financial advisor, you'll have more money to work with.

Shop around now for the best deals, because you will certainly find some. Wealthy relatives and rich uncles are ready to help out if you need extra spending money. You could receive an inheritance too, and accumulate a lot, if you plan wisely. Just don't think this trend is going to last forever. Put some money away for a rainy day; you'll be glad you did.

The Number Eight Year is also a fine time to be thinking about new ways to make money. If you have business skills and would like to operate your own company, now is the time to go after some funding and get started. You'll be surprised at how much you make with little effort. If you currently own a business, you may raise your prices now. Don't take anything for granted or dismiss opportunities; they could come out of the blue to bring you extra money.

Sometimes the Eight Cycle is not consistent. You may enjoy lots of extra spending power one week then feel broke the next. But if you really need cash for something, it will be there.

Many people receive legal settlements during this period. Ss-cholarship funding and lots of credit card applications arrive in the mail! Don't be afraid to speak up now for a raise or to apply for a loan. Let people know that your skills are valuable. Your talents, time and energy are worth a lot.

NUMBER NINE YEAR

This year wraps up your entire 9-year cycle. Here, we deal with the karma of the past 8 years—the lessons you still need to learn or debts you need to repay.

Anything you didn't do or handle correctly in the previous cycles, you must address now. You have no choice.

Some people fear the approaching Nine Year. Others are not affected at all, because they have lived their cycles correctly.

Many times, the past will come back to haunt you. For instance, if you ended a relationship badly with your ex, you'll probably meet up to make amends. Likewise, if you've been waiting for an old lover to kiss and make up, this is the year he or she could waltz back into your life.

This is also a time when some of you could be graduating, divorcing, ending friendships, moving or quitting a dead-end job.

Your Number Nine Year doesn't always bring bad luck, but most of us don't follow the straight and narrow. There are usually some things we must contend with. The least you'll experience is a feeling of being "held back". It's as if you can't get ahead, no matter how hard you push. The universe is telling you to slow down. Allow yourself time to reflect. You'll be up and running when the Number One Year hits on your next birthday.

THIRTEEN

Reading Your Palm

The Future is in the Palm of Your Hand

Your palms have a story to tell . . . a story about you, your life and where it is headed. The art of palmistry has been studied and used for centuries to predict health, financial success and love. These days, anyone who can read a book can learn to read their own palm. To read yours, here's what you'll need?

A magnifying glass
Pen and paper
Two clean hands

When studying the palms, you should read both, but most people read their dominant hand. If you're right-handed, read your right hand. If you're a lefty, use your left hand. The non-dominant palm shows what you *could* have made out of your life. Sometimes it represents your potential. The dominant hand represents your future and reveals all sorts of wonderful things about your character, personality, how many times you'll be married, how many kids you'll have and much more.

Did you know that the lines in your palm change? Just because you read your palm once doesn't mean it stays the same. As you age and experience new things, the lines will change. The lines reflect new attitudes and talents you've developed. Lines can grow longer, shorten and even disappear altogether! If you were to read your palm every 6 months or so, you'd be surprised at how many lines have changed. There also are some lines that don't appear until you reach middle-age.

Most kids under age 10 don't have a fate line. There are major lines in your palms, like the life and heart line. And there are many minor lines, such as the fate line. The minor ones develop as you get older and experience life. Then, as people age, they lose some of their lines or the lines shorten. When elderly people suffer memory loss, the lines in their palms seem to fade or blur. If someone's hand is paralyzed, it has no lines, yet the palm of his non-paralyzed hand does.

Let's find out more about you. What can your palm reveal about the future?

This diagram will show the major lines in your palm. They are:

The Life Line
The Heart Line
The Head Line

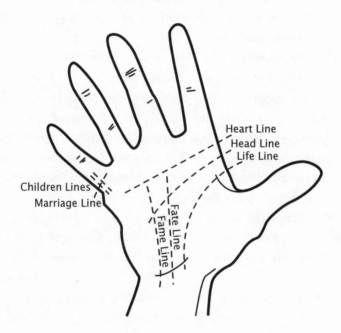

If you can find these three lines, you can learn the basics of palm reading. These three major lines help you understand a lot about your personality. Remember to read both palms. Your dominant hand will show you the person you have become because of your childhood upbringing and life circumstance. Your other hand shows what kind of person you could have become and maybe even your karma! Further study could provide you with a sneak peak into past lives and the lessons brought over into this one!

EXAMINING YOUR LINES

Here are some key questions to ask yourself:
1. Are your lines deep or shallow?
2. Are your lines wide or narrow?
3. Are there breaks, forks or other indentations in your lines?
4. Are your lines curved or straight?
5. Where do the lines begin and end?

Notes: The head and the heart lines are read from the inside of the palm near the thumb, to the outside of the palm. The heart line is read the opposite way, from the outside little finger to the inside.

The lines also show you an approximate time in your life for things to happen. You can "age" your lines very simply. Divide each line into seven even sections. Each section represents about 10 years of life. Most people will probably live longer, but we'll use 10-year increments. This will not give you an exact year or date but will give you a range. For example; childhood, young adult, old age, etc.

PALM MARKING DEFINITIONS

Branch—A line that branches off of the original line. It usually means a change or new direction. Starting a new project, moving, a new job, etc.

Crosses—Two lines that intersect on a line mean a struggle or hard times. The event or problem will be one you will not likely forget.

Stars—Mean your dreams will come true. Stars mostly show up on the head or heart lines.

Triangles—A good sign. These tell of happy times ahead.

Breaks—Breaks means endings. If there is a break in your heart line, it could mean the end of a relationship. If the broken line begins in a new direction, it means a complete change and a new love interest.

Netting or meshing—Means stress and usually shows up when you're tired and overwhelmed by life.

Your Heart Line

Your heart line, also known as your "love line", is the very top line in the palm. It starts a bit below your little finger and runs across the palm. The heart line reveals information about your love life and how you deal with emotions. It predicts the ups and downs of your relationships over the next 70 years or so.

NOW, LET'S INTERPRET YOUR HEART LINE.

—Small branches that swing upward from the heart line, mean you will have a happy love life and lots of good friends. The more upward branches you have, the more popular you will be.

—Branches in a downward position mean heartbreak or disappointment in love and friendships.

—If the heart line curves up, you fall in love fast. You wear your heart on your sleeve and can get hurt easily. But you'll rebound quickly and be off on the next conquest! Romance is very important. You are a passionate person. The bigger the curve, the more romantic you are inclined to be!

—If the heart line is straight or has a small curve, you are cautious and not so apt to fall head-over-heels in love. You are loyal and make a good partner. You're a little too logical at times and will need to make an extra effort to be affectionate.

—Long, straight heart lines mean you are very intense, jealous and possessive. You give 110 % in a relationship, but can be a little controlling.

—If your heart line turns down at the end, this means you can be moody and hard to deal with. You won't find this example often. Most heart lines curve upward. But if you're dating someone who's heart line turns down, you can expect the relationship to be stormy! If you have such a line, you may want to change some of your attitudes about love and be more optimistic.

Your Head Line

The head line is directly below the heart line. It is above the life line. Your head line will tell you about your talents, ambitions, intellect and natural abilities.

The head line is read from the pointer (index) finger, next to your thumb, across your palm.

LET'S INTERPRET YOUR HEAD LINE:

—If your head line is cut deep and you can see it clearly, you're very intelligent. Deep lines also show confidence. A shallow line means you're intuitive but less confident. You could question yourself a lot. There is a tendency to be sentimental.

—If there's meshing or netting on this line, you need to learn to relax. You push yourself too hard. By aging this line, one can determine an approximate time to avoid stress.

—If your head line is straight, you're apt to be logical. The mind will be strong throughout your entire life. Your memory will be good.

—A curved head line means you're creative. You can be enthusiastic but sometimes act before you think. You possess strong writing and acting skills.

—If your head line has a deep dip in it, you could be too sensitive. You have to learn to follow through on things you start. One can get all excited about a project, quickly lose interest and drop it.

—If the head line ends in a fork, you see both sides of a coin. If there is not a fork, you believe your way is the only way to do things!

—If there are a lot of forks running throughout the head line, these represent many changes in your life.

—Large branches at the end of the line mean you have two different personalities. You can be serious yet fun-loving, saucy but sweet, naughty but nice!

—If the head line ends in a fork with three branches, you are psychic. Not too many people have this configuration, but it's commonly seen in the palms of psychics and mediums.

—Branches in the head line represent events in your life. Downward branches mean troubling times. Upward branches show happy events and successful periods.

—If your head line merges with the life line, family and society will have a great influence on your life. If it doesn't, you'll be independent and a bit of a rebel.

—The wider the space between the head and the life lines, the more independent you are.

—If the head and life line merge together and a mesh appears at the beginning of these lines, you've experienced childhood trauma or crisis. If the meshing continues down the lines, it means you are still affected by things that happened in younger years.

—The longer your head line, the longer it takes you to make a decision. A shorter head line means you'll make up your mind more quickly and will not be as indecisive. However, there is a tendency to be impulsive.

The Life Line

The life line is the last major line. It starts on the inside of the palm above your thumb, and runs to the base of the palm.

People always assume that the life line predicts your life span. Not so! It really has to do with physical well being. If you have a short life line, don't panic! It doesn't mean you'll die young. Remember, lines grow and change as you do. The life line will tell you about health, energy levels and lifestyle changes.

NOW LET'S INTERPRET YOUR LIFE LINE:

—Very deep lines mean you have lots of energy. You don't need as much rest as other folks and are probably impatient with slow people. You are a bundle of energy.

—A shallow life line belongs to someone who has low physical energy. They are apt to get tired quickly. If you have a shallow line here, make sure to get at least 8 hours of sleep a night. Take your vitamins too, because you could be prone to catching colds.

—Breaks in your life line can indicate illness or accidents. If your line breaks off and starts in another direction, it means you will overcome that difficulty.

—If there is a sudden break in the life line and then it starts up elsewhere, there will be a dramatic change in your life, perhaps even a lifestyle change.

—Branches and breaks on the life line can give you insight of things to come, but that can change. You can change things. We all have the power of free will. So, if you know there could be a major crisis in the near future, plan for it and be prepared!

—If you have branches shooting upward, this means you will achieve your goals. Downward branches mean disappointments in your ambitions. *Breaks* in the life line have more to do with physical problems, while *branches* have to do with emotional issues.

—A fork in your life line shows that a decision needs to be made and it will be a major one.

—Chains on your life line mean physical problems or minor health concerns. If you have a lot of chains, you could have allergies.

—If you have a curve that almost forms a circle from the inside of the thumb to the base of the palm, you like things peaceful. You're easygoing.

—If your life line swings wide, you love to travel. If it runs completely across your palm, you won't have an ordinary life. You will need change and new adventure to be happy. A wide line, without much of a curve, means you are content with the simple pleasures that life has to offer.

—If the life line clings to the thumb, you are a cautious person. You probably won't move far from home. Family and old friends are very important.

—If your life line curves widely around the thumb, you'll want to try everything once! You love nice things.

The Minor Lines

Minor lines do not appear on everyone's hands. You may not find any on your palms. Some of the lines do not develop until later in life. Others may never develop at all because they don't represent part of your personality. These lines include the marriage, children, fate and fame lines. Keep checking every few months though, one of these lines could turn up and you'll want to know exactly what it means!

The Fate Line

Of all the minor lines, I feel that the fate line is the most important. It is also known as the karma or destiny line. It runs from the bottom of your hand through the middle. It will show you what you're supposed to do with your life—your true purpose and path. It is important to read the fate lines in both palms. Your dominant hand will show how your fate line has changed because of the events in your life. The non-dominant hand will show what your destiny was when you born.

LET'S EXAMINE YOUR FATE LINE MORE CLOSELY:

—If the fate line on your dominant hand is well defined, you are an independent person. If you have a prominent fate line in your other hand but not in the dominant one, it means you have not used or reached your potential yet. The fate line can also tell you what career or job path you may excel in.

—If the fate line runs up the middle of your palm to your index (pointer) finger, you will be very ambitious in your career.

You'd make a good business person, lawyer or law enforcement agent.

—If the fate line moves straight up towards the middle finger, you are a born leader. You would be good in politics, business and supervising, managing or teaching others.

—A fate line that lines up under a ring finger, reveals that you are a dramatic and creative person. You'd make a great actor, musician or artist.

—If your fate line leans toward your little finger, journalism, writing, broadcasting and teaching are natural abilities.

—If your fate line starts in the middle of your palm, expect to become successful a little later in life. You may take a decade or so to decide what it is you want to do.

—If the fate line starts at the bottom of the palm and ends midway up, you'll start working at a young age and retire early.

—If your fate line doesn't start until it reaches the heart line, your love life will always be more important than work. Your world will center around those you love.

—If the fate line is deep, this means you are determined to succeed. Nothing will stand in the way of your goals.

—If there are a lot of breaks, there may be difficulties and career losses. Breaks also mean different types of employment. You could bounce from one job to another.

—A line that is long and runs from the very bottom of the hand to the base of the fingers is the sign of a workaholic.

—A fate line that ends in a fork means there will be a big decision or career change at some point in your life.

—A star at the bottom of the fate line means you will find success and happiness in your chosen career.

—For those who have no fate line, it merely means no set path has been made. You will create your own.

Fame Line

Do you have star quality? Will all of your hard efforts pay off? Will your name be in lights? Not surprising, the fame line is not found in everyone's hand. But if you have one, it runs from the middle of your hand to the ring finger. Your fame line is on the outside of your fate line. It is usually fainter and harder to read. I suggest using your magnifying glass to see it more clearly.

LET'S INTERPRET YOUR FAME LINE:

—A long fame line suggests that everyone adores you.

—If the fame line starts on your life line, you have star quality. Yes, you could be a VIP!

—A fame line that branches off from your fate line means you'll be famous because of your career.

—When the fame line starts from your head line, you could receive recognition because of a book you write or an invention. You will be recognized because of your hard work.

—If the fame line starts at the heart line, you could marry someone who is well respected. It doesn't mean you'll marry Tom Cruise or Julia Roberts . . . but there is a chance! The people you date or associate with, could be well known.

Marriage Lines

Marriage lines are short horizontal lines under your little finger, almost on the edge of the hand. The lines that go up and down and through the marriage lines are called children lines. They represent how many kids you're likely to have. (See the next section for more information on children lines.) You will need a magnifying glass to read these. The marriage lines can tell you how many trips down the aisle you'll make, and other interesting things about committed relationships.

LET'S INTERPRET THE MARRIAGE LINES:

—Short, feathered lines mean short relationships that go nowhere. Longer, deep lines mean steady relationships are in your future.

—A single deep line stands for a long term commitment or one marriage.

—Two deep lines equal two long-term marriages.

—If you have several lines, you can expect a lot of relationships and commitments. Usually the number of lines represents the number of marriages.

—If the marriage line ends in a fork, a marriage will end in divorce.

Children Lines

Children lines go up and down though the marriage lines. If you are very young, these lines may be very faint or not show up at all ... just yet.

If you have found lines here, count the lines. This is likely the number of kids you will have.

There are many more minor lines in your palms with fascinating stories to tell and secrets to reveal. Palmistry is like your own personal road map. But remember, you still drive the car! Your life's direction is ultimately up to you.

FOURTEEN

The Art of Tarot

★ ★ ★ The ancient art of tarot reading has been used for centuries all over the world. In the past century, tarot reading has been looked upon as more of a new age form of divination, but there's nothing "new" about it. The tarot can be traced back to the eleventh century in the Far East. These cards were modeled more after a regular deck of playing cards than the tarot sets we see today are. Gypsies used the tarot for years and are said to have brought the cards into Europe, where they enjoyed great popularity. In the middle ages, dozens of different types of tarot card sets were designed.

Even though the tarot underwent many facelifts and artistic changes, its message remains the same, even to this day. There is a massive amount of ancient, spiritual wisdom alive in the cards.

The tarot combines belief systems such as the Hebrew Cabala, astrology and numerology. Today, you can walk into any new age book store and find hundreds of different tarot designs. There are Goddess cards, Native American tarot, animal tarot, Halloween tarot, and even baseball tarot card sets. They may all have different pictures but the meanings in the cards remain the same.

The tarot is nothing to be scared of; it is to be respected. Taken seriously and considered a sacred tool, it can help you unlock some of the mysteries of life and what lies before you. There are 78 cards in the tarot deck including the 22 major *arcana* cards and 56 minor *arcana*. *Arcana* means "profound secrets". In this chapter you will learn what each of the major arcana cards mean and how to give a yes/no reading and a basic reading.

WHAT KIND OF CARDS SHOULD YOU GET?

If you're serious about learning and reading tarot, you'll want to get a good, high-quality deck of cards. As I mentioned, there are possibly hundreds of different types of tarot cards on the market today. How do you choose? I suggest you go to a bookstore or a new age boutique that offers a good selection. Then pick through the cards that you are drawn to the most. What appeals to you? If there are sample decks already open, look through them. Ask if you can open a deck you are particularly interested in. Feel how the deck fits in your hand. Fan the cards out. What feelings do you get from them? Do you feel good about the cards? Shuffle them. Do you still feel drawn to them? If the answer is yes, it's the right deck for you!

HOW TO TAKE CARE OF YOUR CARDS

Your cards should never be used as a game or toy. They represent sacred symbols. Never let anyone play with or use your cards. Do not lend them out. You can show people the deck, but don't let them use it. You should be the only person to handle your deck and read it. Your energy is intertwined with the cards once you claim the deck as your own.

Anyone else's energy could lessen or dampen the effect, the strength and accuracy the deck will have in your readings. When you are not using the deck, wrap it in silk, cotton or another natural fabric. Some people keep their cards in a wooden box.

TO PREPARE FOR A READING

Before giving a reading, I suggest you set the stage or create the right mood. Some people burn incense or candles. Others play soft, flowing music to create a relaxed atmosphere. Before beginning a reading, I always envision a beautiful white light surrounding me and the person I am reading for. The white light is a light of protection and peace. Some say a little prayer beforehand. Your mind should be clear and relaxed. You should never give a reading when you are upset, sick, angry, tired or in a bad mood.

CREATE A LEARNER'S DECK

One idea, I'd like to share with those just learning the meaning of the cards, is to purchase two decks, so that you can make one your "learner's deck". All decks come with a small instruction booklet containing the meanings of each individual card. Some sets come with a larger book with pictures of the cards and their descriptions.

I suggest that, on your "learner's deck", you write the upright position meaning on the top of the corresponding card and the reversed position on the bottom. Then, as you practice, you won't have to look up the meaning each time in your booklet. You'll memorize each card easily this way and eventually won't need the learner's deck. *The upright position is when the card is drawn upright; the reversed position means the card is drawn upside down.*

HOW TO CUT THE CARDS

You will want to shuffle your cards first. Cut the deck with your left hand into three piles. Then pick up the piles with your left hand, put them together and fan the cards out on a table.

Some readers just fan all of the cards out on a table and mix them up. Then they'll choose cards they are drawn to. Other readers shuffle the cards like an ordinary deck of playing cards and fan them out. The client picks cards they are drawn to. Both ways are fine. One is no better than the other. This boils down to personal preference—but choosing the cards you want to read is important.

You should take great care not to hurry to choose cards. Take your time, slow down, breathe! Run your hand over the cards. Which cards are calling to you? These cards are the ones you should pick up. These will have special and deep meaning.

When you choose the cards, pick them up with your left hand if you are right-handed. If you're left-handed, use your right. This is a magic moment. Choosing your cards is almost like a ritual. If you honor the process, your reading will be accurate. The cards will honor you. There are just as many layouts as there are tarot card types. We will only concern ourselves with three of them right now. The easiest one to use is the yes/no reading.

Yes/No Reading

The simplest way to get an answer using the major arcana cards is to ask a yes-or-no question. Take the 22 major arcana cards out of the deck and put the others aside. Shuffle the cards and think of a question over and over in your mind. You can ask it out loud if you wish. After you shuffle the cards, fan them out on the table and pick up one card that you are drawn to. If a card drops out of the deck while you are shuffling, you should read that one. Look in the booklet that came with your cards for a physical description.

Ask a question that can be answered simply. Do not attempt to ask a long one that will require a detailed answer; those types of questions can be saved for the longer layout reading. Phrase your question like this:

> *Will I be dating someone this year?*
> *Will my job improve?*
> *Will I get a new car?*

This reading will not give you times when things are likely to happen. Do not ask the same question over and over, even if you don't like the answer. Do not ask the same question twice in a 24-hour period. Accept the answer and decide what on the best steps to take to deal with what the card has told you.

After you have drawn your card, look up its meaning in the next few chapters. You'll be able to determine whether the card is favorable or unfavorable. For example, if you were to ask the tarot, "Will I be dating soon?" and you drew the Lovers card, the obvious answer would be yes, a new relationship is on the way.

The Three Card Spread (past, present and future)

Another simple layout to learn is the past, present and future reading. Shuffle the cards, fan them out and pick three cards. The first card you pick should be laid to your left. It represents your past, what has already happened and what you know to be true. The second card you draw is to be placed directly in front of you. This is your present card and deals with current conditions and circumstances around you right now. The third card is placed to the right and will tell you what you can expect to happen in the near future or the outcome of the event or circumstance.

Maria Shaw's 12-Month Spread

This layout is good for timing events, and if you wish to do an in-depth, longer reading. Shuffle the cards, fan them out and pick 12 cards. The first card you draw should be the first one you read, and so on.

Place six cards in a row and six cards in another row beneath the first set, face down. Turn the first card over. This card will tell you what is likely to happen during the month of the reading (the current month). In the book, read the information about this card.

Flip the second card over. It will tell you what to expect next month. The third card will give you insight on 3 months from now, and so on.

Let's look at the meanings of the 22 major arcana cards

0. Fool	XI. Justice
I. Magician	XII. The Hanged Man
II. The High Priestess	XIII. Death
III. Empress	XIV. Temperance
IV. The Emperor	XV. The Devil
V. The Hierophant	XVI. The Tower
VI. The Lovers	XVII. The Star
VII. The Chariot	XVIII. The Moon
VIII. Strength	XIX. The Sun
IX. The Hermit	XX. Judgment
X. The Wheel of Fortune	XXI. The World

0. THE FOOL

Upright Position

If the Fool falls upright in one of your tarot layouts, it means you can expect a brand new cycle of life to begin. Perhaps you are starting a new job, getting married or moving far away. You will have doubts about a new direction, but don't worry, things are likely to turn out in your favor. Just remember to trust your inner voice. This is a period in which you could be misled by someone. So, listen to your intuition.

This is an exciting time but it can also bring unexpected challenges. You may be faced with a decision to make. However, you must take risks in order to get ahead and succeed. In love, there could be a relationship on the horizon. In the job market, take a leap of faith and apply for a top position.

Reversed Position

The meaning of this card, in the reversed position, warns that you must not proceed with current plans. You need to stop and analyze what is going on in your life. You could be taking the wrong road or making foolish decisions. There will be confusion. Do not rush into anything, for there are problems you didn't anticipate. You will long for excitement or change, but your current choices are not the right ones. Be cautious. Play a waiting game.

I. THE MAGICIAN

Upright Position

The Magician represents the power of your imagination. You have the great ideas and inner power to manifest your own destiny. This card shows up when you are creating a new idea or opportunity in your life. You will be filled with enthusiasm and learn to master new skills. Any project you are starting goes well. Like the magician, you have extraordinary powers to make your dreams come true now.

Reversed Position

There could be someone around you who is two-faced. Beware of so-called friends. They could be hidden enemies. You may feel tired or confused. Do not bow to pressure, but listen to your own inner thoughts. Stay true to who you are and things will work out for the best. There may be a few missed opportunities because you lack self confidence. This troubling time will pass. You need to learn to trust your own instincts more. There may be problems in your personal and professional life.

II. THE HIGH PRIESTESS

Upright Position

The High Priestess will show up in a reading when you need to develop and trust your own psychic powers. She could also be warning you that a situation is not what it appears to be. There could be deception around you. You may have more dreams now. They could have prophetic meanings. Write these dreams down. Take them seriously. Your subconscious mind is trying to get your attention. If you have a question or a concern that you just can't seem to resolve, it may take a month until all of your answers will be revealed. You must practice patience until then.

Reversed Position

You may feel as if you're on an emotional roller coaster ride. You need to stay calm and not overreact to situations. Do not act quickly or impulsively now, because you may regret your actions later. There will be friends and family members pushing your buttons. Remain cool, calm and collected.

III. THE EMPRESS

Upright Position

You're coming into a period of great personal achievement. You will have lots of luck in relationships and at work. Projects that you begin now will flourish and grow. At work, your boss will notice your abilities. Your love life is fantastic! You'll look and feel good. This is a pregnancy card too, so you or someone you know well could have a baby!

Reversed Position

You may feel as if you have hit a road block. You're working very hard to achieve something but nothing seems to be moving forward. This is a frustrating period. If you draw the Empress card in this position, it is important to keep believing that things will turn out for the best. Don't give up. Have faith.

IV. THE EMPEROR

Upright Position

This card will give you great wisdom and insight on your question. You can achieve much success now. Move forward with courage and conviction. Doors will easily open. If you are looking for love, this card foretells a new romance right around the corner. Your dreams can become reality, especially if you are willing to work hard on your goals and be open to the new opportunities the Emperor wants to bring you.

Reversed Position

Feeling down or discouraged about something? Probably. You may even feel like giving up! There are people around who won't give you a break. You may apply for a new job and not get it. You may ask someone out on a date and be turned down. There could be danger, frustration and jealousy around you. You'll be learning a great deal about your own strength and what you are made of!

V. THE HIEROPHANT

Upright Position

If you are searching for an answer to a major problem, this card is telling you to take things slowly. You need to create some sort of discipline or order in your life, so things will run smoothly. Stay with a regular routine. Don't veer too far off the beaten path. Rather than argue, fight, worry or be anxious, take the time to listen, to be quiet and perhaps to meditate. Your answer will come from deep within you. If your question is about love, you either need to make a commitment to someone or break off a relationship. At work, get promises in writing. This card is also telling you to get more rest. Go to bed earlier.

Reversed Position

When reversed, this card means chaos and problems. You want to break free. You are tired of being a goody two-shoes. Life seems so boring! Friendships and relationships may be in turmoil. You may be attracted to the wild side of life. Be careful. You could be stepping into dangerous territory.

VI. THE LOVERS

Upright Position

When you draw this card, a new relationship is coming into your life, or you are in one, or you need to make a decision regarding love very soon. Your intuition will be strong and you'll be using your heart rather than your head to make decisions. Sometimes, an old flame returns. You will feel strong emotions toward someone. A new love affair may lead to a serious commitment.

Reversed Position

The Lovers card reversed means that you'll be going through a difficult period in your relationships. You may have to make a choice you don't want to. There will be rocky times ahead. Yes, there could be a break-up, tears and sorrow.

VII. THE CHARIOT

Upright Position

If you draw the Chariot, it means you are in a period of change. You may have been struggling with a situation in the recent past, but will have the freedom to move forward now. You should have learned a great deal in the last several months and now realize that nothing is black and white. Nothing stays the same. This is a cycle in which you are moving away from the past and into the future. There'll be new friends, new jobs, a new relationship and maybe even a move. You will succeed now. This card also means you could take a trip.

Reversed Position

If you're traveling or are considering a trip, there may be delays or confusion. You may be lacking in self confidence at this time. There are people around who are trying to control you. You need to be calm and silent. There could be defeat and failure. Do not make any major decisions now. Just sit and listen. This period will pass in a few weeks.

VIII. STRENGTH

Upright Position

You will be able to solve any problem that comes your way, if you use a gentle touch rather than force. Be kind and sympathetic in your dealings with friends and family. Love is ever powerful. It can heal all. This card is also telling you to love yourself. Treat yourself now. You probably have been overwhelmed lately and there hasn't been much time to rest. Slow down a bit! You can gain much strength and wisdom at this time. Your confidence levels will improve and if there are any difficult people around you, they will be nicer.

Reversed Position

You may not feel well. This is a period of low energy. You may catch a bad cold. Get more rest. If you're burning the candles at both ends, exhaustion will set in. Try not to overdo, and go to bed earlier!

IX. THE HERMIT

Upright Position

When you draw this card, you have just come out of a period of much activity; now it's time to stop and rest a while. If you are seeking an answer to a problem, you will not get it right away. You are supposed to retreat for a while, think it over and then the answer will come. The Hermit represents your inner self, and by getting in touch with your spiritual side, answers come easily and light your way. It would also be wise to see a therapist or counselor at this time.

Reversed Position

The Hermit warns you to be careful. Be cautious in all of your dealings. There are important messages around you. You inner voice is trying to talk to you. Your friends, and loved ones are giving you good advice. Heed it! You could feel angry now and reject any offers of help, even from your mate and loved ones. Take the time to look at the other side of the coin. Things will improve shortly.

X. THE WHEEL OF FORTUNE

Upright Position

The Wheel of Fortune means you have ended a major cycle of life and will soon start another one. You are especially lucky now. Things will fall into your lap. Be open to trying new ventures. You'll be amazed at all of the wonderful opportunities that lie before you! The wheel is turning in a good direction. Trust that everything will turn out wonderful and be for your highest good. Expect money or opportunities to come your way!

Reversed Position

You'll feel as if you are going backwards. Nothing seems to be moving forward. It's as if a dark cloud is hanging over your head. There will be delays and frustrations, but things do not stay this way for long. Know that this is a temporary position and things will start moving again. This is not a favorable time for starting anything new.

XI. JUSTICE

Upright Position

You find things fall in your favor easily. You are being instructed by this card to act with honesty and fairness in all of your dealings now. Whatever you put out, will come back to you! Sometimes this card represents a marriage, a new relationship or a wonderful friendship. There may be legal concerns at this time, but don't worry, things will turn out okay.

Reversed Position

People will not treat you fairly. You may feel like a victim and probably are. You notice that people are working against you rather than with you. On a mundane level, this is a time to avoid legal matters. Stay out of court. You may also work hard on a project and not get the proper credit. Some things will seem unfair. Friends will argue more. You desperately want to restore peace and balance in your life now.

XII. THE HANGED MAN

Upright Position

This is a period in which you could experience sadness or sacrifice. You may have to let someone go or give up something you thought was important. However, it will not be as bad or as frightening as one might think. You could also feel that you are in "limbo", waiting for something to happen. Creative work, such as art, writing and music, can help you get through this confusing time.

Reversed Position

This card in this position is actually a good thing! It means there is an end in sight to your frustration, suffering or crisis. A lot of your questions will be answered. You do not have to go to great lengths to see changes now. You won't have to give up anything. You are free!

XIII. DEATH

Special note: People mistake this card for meaning a physical death, that someone close to them is dying. They look frightened if they draw it. They feel it's the worst card in the entire deck. Some even think the card means they will die! Not so. Death means the breaking down and rebuilding of something. There is a major change coming, but look at the sun beyond in the distance. There is good coming.

Upright Position

The Death card means a positive change. You will be letting go of old, worn-out habits, negative friends and situations. You will start a new life or new direction. Thoughts and beliefs will change. Even though you may go through a period of self doubt, many new and wonderful opportunities await. Press forward. Let go of the past and be open to what the future will bring you. There will be much happiness.

Reversed Position

The Death card reversed means there will be a "block" in your life that you can't seem to overcome. You may be the cause of the blockage. Or you may not want to let go of something or someone that is negative. Sometimes we suppress our feelings. We hang onto old beliefs and negative thinking. You could be afraid to let go of a lousy group of friends or an addiction. Fear will hold you back. Be more open and things will change for the better.

XIV. TEMPERANCE

Upright Position

You have recently gone through a period of turmoil and hard work. You are now open and ready to receive the bounties of the universe. If something seems to be missing in your life, or if there is a feeling of emptiness, soon you will feel light-hearted and full of joy. When you draw this card, you can land the perfect job, discover new friends and even meet your soul mate! If you were depressed in the past, there was a reason for it . . . to reach this point in your life and appreciate what the world has to offer. Your life will be in perfect harmony and balance very shortly.

Reversed Position

This card reversed means there is no balance in your life right now. You are so busy, you can't focus. It's as if you are trying to accomplish too much too soon. Therefore, nothing gets done. You're headed for major burnout. This is a difficult time and you'll be tested. But these tests will make you stronger. The way you look at life and your belief system may change a lot too.

XV. THE DEVIL

Upright Position

You'll be obsessed with a situation or someone. This is not healthy. You could be a bit frightened too. Many times, fear comes from being insecure and not wanting to let go. Perhaps you are dating someone and are fearful they will break the relationship off. You may know this is for the best but are so taken with him or her, that you hang on out of desperation. You could be too obsessed with making money and take on more work than you can handle. This card is here to advise you that true happiness comes from within. You may make a wrong choice if this card comes up in the spread. Do not misuse any powers of manipulation, because they may come back on you.

Reversed Position

The reversed Devil card is good. It means you are free! You may have just gone through a struggling period and come out a winner. You will no longer be held back or kept a prisoner. One can walk away from a bad relationship, confident there will be good times soon and that love is right around the corner.

XVI. THE TOWER

Upright Position

Expect the unexpected to happen. The Tower card represents dramatic and amazing changes in your life. Things that have been building up over a period of time, may now create a major explosion. The actual change will happen quickly. You could break off a relationship, quit a job without giving notice or argue with a mate or lover. There will be upheavals in your life. Watch out for stress and anxiety soon. After the dust settles, you'll clearly see why this chaos had to happen. There are lessons to learn.

Reversed Position

Do you feel as if something big is going to happen? You know a change is coming but aren't sure when? The reversed Tower means that, yes, there is an upheaval, but it is expected and you can accept and manage the outcome well. There could be more surprises, twists and turns over the next few weeks, but you'll be able to handle them. This could actually be a very productive phase of your life. Be open to accepting these changes. They're usually for the better.

XVII. THE STAR

Upright Position

There are new adventures coming into your life. You will be eager and hopeful about your circumstances now. Things will change for the better. Expect good to come to you. Friends will support you. If you need help in any area of life, do not be afraid to ask, because many want to offer assistance. Doors open up. There are new opportunities as never before. You are being recognized and adored! This is a great card for showing off your talents and abilities too!

Reversed Position

The Star reversed means that you are full of indecisiveness and doubt. You have lost all faith in yourself. You are not ambitious, and feel as if life is meaningless. This is a temporary state of mind. The best thing to do is to meditate, practice uplifting affirmations and just wait. This dark cloud will lift, but you must push yourself to keep going. You have a choice to either smile or frown. If you smile, the light within you will glow and things will turn around. Do not allow yourself to get down.

XVIII. THE MOON

Upright Position

Your sixth sense is heightened and you could become extremely psychic. This card also means that you are tired and overwhelmed by life. There could be deceitful people around. Don't trust everyone. There's a lot of rumor and gossip, too. The moon phases take a month so expect changes to occur in the next 30 days. You will need all of your energy to deal with the negativity. Listen to your intuition. Get readings from others if it's hard to interpret your dreams or visions yourself.

Reversed Position

You will feel more at ease soon. There is less deception around you now. The ups and downs of life are coming to an end. If someone was lying to you in the past, you will be able to see his true colors clearly. You are no longer in the dark, so move forward with a clear conscience and determination. Don't let anything stand in your way.

XIX. THE SUN

Upright Position

The Sun is shining upon *you*! There will be success and fulfillment. You need to take the first steps to achieve your goals now. If you have a new project or idea, go for it. You will feel a sense of rebirth and a burst of energy. You cannot fail! The world is waiting for you and granting your every wish and desire. Use this time to make progress and positive changes.

Reversed Position

You may feel defeated soon. A goal or project you had been working on, doesn't turn out as you had hoped. Someone else may bask in your limelight or get more recognition. Your time is coming, but not right now, so you need to "keep the faith". Avoid getting depressed or involved in negative thinking patterns.

XX. JUDGMENT

Upright Position

The Judgment card is a final-decision card. You will make up your mind about something. Even if there have been difficulties in the recent past, much progress can be made now. The choices that lie before you are quite clear. Great changes can occur if you are willing to release old fears. When you draw this card, nothing is impossible.

Reversed Position

You feel disheartened and discouraged. You may think the dream you are chasing is not within your reach, or that the road you're on is leading nowhere. You may indeed have to change your ideals and goals now. Don't let negative thinking hold you back. There is a reason and a season for everything.

XXI THE WORLD

Upright Position

When we draw this card, we must recognize that our focus is on change. We must look at changing something about our life in order to succeed. Then success will be imminent. This is one of the luckiest cards in the entire deck.

Reversed Position

There is a possibility of failure. You must follow through with projects you start. Don't give up on a situation too soon. Look at ways you can consciously change something to make it better or more profitable.

FIFTEEN

Sweet Dreams

★ ★ ★ Interpreting dreams can be a wonderful hobby. Think of a dream as your own private movie screening. Sometimes you play the leading role. Other times you're just an observer. These "movies" can be romantic, mysterious, action-oriented, scary or just plain bizarre. If you dream a lot, you may be curious to find out what your dreams are trying to tell you. Your subconscious mind is trying to grab your attention. Perhaps there's important news coming, a crisis or a story to unravel. Maybe a prediction of forthcoming events.

You can easily learn to interpret your dreams and even your nightmares. Dreaming is one way your subconscious mind can get you to listen. It has important things to tell you. Some people get psychic impressions through their dreams. Others may dream only when being forewarned about something. Some people say they never dream. They do. They just don't remember.

We all dream. Sometimes we can recall our dreams vividly. Other times we wake up and can't remember a thing. Seldom do we know or understand the real significance of our dreams. A lot of them have hidden meanings. They could be prophetic in some way—give us a glimpse into our future. Some are so strange that they don't make any sense.

You never know what or who you'll see in a dream. Our friends and family members may make an appearance. Even loved ones who have passed on. This chapter will unlock some of the mysteries of "your dreaming mind". Those born under the sign of Pisces dream a lot. This is one way they receive psychic messages. It is important for Pisces to learn the art of interpretation. However, all members of the zodiac can benefit from understanding dreams.

The first thing to bear in mind is that there are two distinctly different types of dreams; prophetic and recurring. **Prophetic dreams** are those that can give us a glimpse into our future. They usually occur during the deepest part of our night's sleep which is usually between about 1 a.m. to 5 a.m. These are the dreams you will want to keep track of, record in a dream journal and attempt to interpret.

Recurring dreams are those you have over and over again. The same theme is present. When I was younger, from about age 7 to 18, I had the same dream every so often. Burglars were breaking into my house and I was desperately trying to climb out of my bedroom window and run across the street to my neighbor's home. I felt safe there. Sometimes, I awoke before I made it across the street. Other times I was able to reach my neighbor's back door before I woke up. I started keeping track of what was happening in my daily life every time I had this dream.

I found that the dream occurred when I was intimidated by someone or something. For example, I'd have a difficult interview coming up and the dream would occur. I was worried about an argument with a friend, went to bed and the dream came up again. So, there I was, running away from something and looking for a safe haven. Now that I am older, I can only recall having this dream three or four times in the past 10 years.

If you are having recurring dreams, there is usually a psychological or emotional reason behind it. It's the subconscious mind telling you that there is something you need to examine or look at within yourself.

There's another kind of dream, too. It doesn't usually have any real significance but you'll remember it vividly and with great detail. This would be the kind of dream you have when you've eaten too much spicy food before going to bed! You've got the munchies at midnight and then all night long you're dreaming mind is on overload. Here's another scenario; You've just watched a scary movie. You're really into it and then you immediately go to bed. Your mind hasn't relaxed or shut down and images similar to the program show up in your dream.

Lets Look at the Different Categories Psychic or Prophetic Dreams Fall Into:

PRECOGNITIVE

I call these psychic dreams. These are the ones you want to write down and take note of. They could come true! They will actually tell you what is coming up. The detail may be a little off, but usually they're close.

My friend Mona had a dream that I was in Italy and was being followed by a handsome, young Italian man. She saw me going into a bookstore and this man kept watching and following close behind me. She didn't feel good about this guy. She said he was kind of creepy. I was all alone. It was during the day and I was indeed, in Italy.

Well, several weeks later, my friend Julie asked me to go to Italy with her, so she wouldn't have to travel alone on a business trip. I was very excited. By this time I had completely forgotten about my friend's dream. While Julie was tied up in meetings, I was walking around Milan all by myself. I went into a huge department store and shopped in the stationary and book section. I noticed this older Italian man staring at me. I felt uncomfortable and went into the children's department across the aisle. He followed. I casually walked into another department. He was right behind me. Then I got on the escalator and went downstairs. He hopped on the escalator too. Off I scurried into the perfume department. He was there! I made a bee-line for the front door of the store, through a crowd of people, hopped on the subway and lost him. My friend's dream was right! But her description of this "stalker" was a little off. He wasn't handsome at all!

This is a good example of a precognitive or prophetic dream. If one of your friends dreams about you, ask them for details. It may be nothing. Perhaps, it's something silly, but it could be important. If you wake up from such a dream, it's best to remember the details early in the day. You remember more as soon as you wake up and over the next few hours. As the day wears on, it's likely you'll lose a lot of information and specific details. Try to write down as much as you can remember, as soon as you wake up.

WARNING DREAMS

Depending on how you feel when you wake up, warning dreams can foretell danger or problems ahead. Dreams such as this, give us prior knowledge to change things or at least be aware that a crisis is coming. Many times we can avoid accidents or problems, if we are given significant warning. Unfortunately, most people don't take heed. They pass their dream off as an overactive imagination. But you really should listen. Your subconscious mind is trying to tell you something.

I have a friend, Char, who one Sunday dreamed of a school that had yellow police tape all around it—the kind you see at crime scenes. She said it worried her because it seemed so real. There were little kids running out of the building and dozens of police cars parked at this school. She was frustrated because she didn't know exactly where the school was located. She felt helpless without more information. She wanted to be able to warn someone, but didn't know who. About 2 days later and 20 miles from where Char lives, a first grader shot another classmate. The little girl died. The tragedy made national news for days. The events that occurred had unfolded in Char's warning dream. It could be considered a prophetic dream too.

There are other people I have counseled who have warning dreams and have been able to stop tragedy before it happened. One man from Michigan saw a motorcycle accident in his dream. He was driving the bike involved in the crash. He woke up sweating! That morning, he placed an ad in the newspaper to sell his bike. He feels he was given a premonition and was able to avoid this accident.

FACTUAL DREAMS

We probably have more factual dreams than any other type. They don't seem to last very long and we get bits and pieces of information though them. Factual dreams are about things we already know about. You could dream of taking a trip (that you took yesterday) or being interviewed for a new job. You could dream of having a conversation with a friend about something that is actually going on in your personal life.

I often dream I am giving readings. I give consultations almost every day, so I guess I do it in my sleep too. I recall one dream in which I was giving a lady a very lengthy and detailed reading. I was mentally tired when I woke up and felt as if I had just completed a 2-hour consultation. I probably had!

INSPIRATION DREAMS

If you are going through a personal problem with a lover, if you are having a difficult time at work or worrying about a family member, an inspiration dream will offer a solution. It will give you an idea of how best to handle the situation. These dreams usually make you feel good. You'll get some answers. Again, remember to write the answers or solutions down right away so you don't forget them.

Here's another idea to help you when you're in the middle of a dilemma: If there's a decision you must make but can't seem to find the right answer, ask yourself the question before you fall asleep at night. Let that be the last thing on your mind as you drift off. During your sleeping hours, your brain has time to process the question or dilemma without battling your emotional side. Your subconscious won't battle your conscious mind. In the morning you'll awake with the right answer. Don't question it! The first thing that comes to your mind is the right answer. It works!

VISITATIONS

I would like to address another type of dream, the visitation. Sometimes, deceased loved ones come to us in a dream. They are likely around us during the day too. Their energy or presence is with us, but we cannot see or even feel it, because our minds are cluttered. When we are asleep, our subconscious is more open to receiving energy and the messages they wish to bring us. This is one of the best times for our loved ones to contact us or make a spiritual connection. Let's distinguish between a simple dream of a loved one and an actual visitation.

A *dream* is something you'll remember when you first wake up in the morning. It will fade over the next few hours and days and then eventually you may have no memory of it at all. A *visitation* is an actual visit from the soul or spirit of someone. It *feels* like a dream but you will remember it vividly. It will stay with you all day, for weeks and months, perhaps even years later.

My father passed on a few years ago. I missed him desperately. Though my dreams, I knew I could connect with him. It was such a wonderful feeling! Actually, before he died, we were talking and I said "Daddy, when you pass on, please come to me in a dream. I won't be scared. Please promise me you will." He kept this promise.

Initially, after someone passes on, their spirit may still linger with family and friends who are grieving. My dad knew I needed him and this is the only way he could reach me. He came many times to me during my sleep over a course of 2 years. I wrote down everything about these dreams. There was a particular one that I absolutely knew was a visitation. My father's spirit had come to visit me. I was still having a hard time with his passing.

We were standing in our kitchen and he hugged me. I actually felt him hug me as he told me everything would be all right. I woke up with such a blessed and joyful feeling! It was wonderful. He had come at other times and talked about some of the difficulties I was going through. He always assured me that everything would be all right. He doesn't come as much as he used to, but it seems that when I ask him and really need to reconnect with my dad, he shows up in a dream. I consider these dreams a special time I can spend with him.

I've noticed when we approach the holiday season or around special milestones, anniversaries and birthdays, loved ones who have passed on make an appearance. It's as if they want to share the special day with you. They want you to know they are near. I have a dream every October about my friend Rick who died almost 8 years ago. His birthday is October 4th.

If there is someone you miss, know that you can still connect with them. Ask them to come to you. You should not do this just for fun or to test the theory, but when you really need that loved one. Many times, departed family and friends will come to us when we're in a major crisis, to offer support, especially if we ask for their help.

Interpreting Your Dreams

As with anything else, the more you practice, the more you will understand and be able to interpret the meanings of your dreams. I suggest keeping a dream journal and getting a good thick interpretation book. Don't invest in one that has a few descriptions with little information in it. Get a large one with great detail.

Generally you are the best interpreter of your dreams. Your subconscious mind will give you answers. But if you having trouble deciphering a meaning, you can always see a reputable dream analyst. A dream interpreter is someone who has studied the meaning of dreams, both the psychological and spiritual meanings, and can explain what your dream is trying to tell you.

Do you know that a bizarre or bad dream may actually be a good omen? Just because you have a scary dream, doesn't always mean it is a bad one. This is another reason to have a detailed dream guide next to your bed.

What happens when two people share the same dream? Let's go back to my dreaming friend, Mona. She was telling me about her neighbor who is in a wheelchair. She had a dream one night that this neighbor was able to walk. In her dream, Mona told her, "Let me help you up. Let's see if you can walk." Back to reality now. The next day, this neighbor called Mona and proceeded to tell her about her own dream. She said Mona was helping her out of the wheelchair and she began walking across the floor! Mona couldn't believe her ears! Hopefully this is a precognitive dream too. But the fact that both women had the same dream, the same night, meant they were both given the same message. Details varied but for the most part, the dreams were the same. Now, for the interesting part, Mona's neighbor recently had an operation and felt movement in her legs!

I find that when two people have the same dream, it's usually a prophetic, one and one person is to share or help the other person through something. The information is so important that, with both people having the same dream, it will not be dismissed or go unnoticed. These types of dreams should be taken seriously and could possibly come true. By all means, interpret these dreams down to their last detail.

The Dream Journal

You can buy dream journals in almost any book store, or you can make your own. They can be very simple. Just a spiral notebook will work. Keep the journal next to your bed along with a pen or pencil. If you don't have time to write in the morning, you can also leave a tape recorder on your night stand so when you wake up you can record what you remember.

Date the journal and begin writing anything and everything you can recall. You can write it in sequence or in bits and pieces. Remember the colors, numbers, faces, places, people, discussions, times and season of the year. Specific details are important. Throughout the day, if you think of anything else, write it down and add it to your journal later. No information is insignificant, but some is more important than others.

Dreams are made up of many elements. There is usually a main theme in every dream. Pick the one thing that stands out in your mind as being the most vivid or important. Analyze and begin to interpret that first. Remember, you are the best interpreter of your dreams.

Ask first, what does it mean to you? Then look up the individual meanings in your dream book. If your dream is full of detail, this means it is very important. If you only remember small bits and pieces and it fades quickly, I wouldn't write much, if anything, in your journal. It may not have any meaning unless it is linked to another dream you've had in the past.

SAMPLE DREAM JOURNAL PAGE

Date_____

1. Describe the dream.

2. How do you feel about the dream (happy?, upset?, confused?)?

3. What was the main theme or element of the dream?

4. What were the minor details of your dream?

5. Were there any special people, places, colors or numbers in your dream?

6. Was there a specific period involved? Current, future or past?

7. Does this dream seem familiar? Did you experience this dream before?

8. Read your dream book and write the interpretation here.

9. With all of the information listed above, what do you think this dream means?

Some Common Dream Interpretations

Here are a few pages of dream interpretations to get you started: But there are thousands and thousands more out there. I suggest getting a large, detailed dream book if you're serious about studying interpretations.

Accident—If you dream of an accident, it is usually meant as a warning. Try to avoid unnecessary travel for a few weeks. Don't drive carelessly. If you can remember what or who was involved in the accident, try to avoid that thing or person for at least the next few days.

Achievement—You will reach a goal and feel very proud of yourself. If you're working on a special project and wonder how it will turn out, this dream is telling you, you'll be successful!

Acne or Pimples—There will be disappointment in a love affair but, better relationships around the bend.

Afraid—To dream of being afraid is often not as bad as it seems. It actually means you will overcome any difficulties in the next few weeks.

Alien—Ever dream of a man from outer space? It means you will make new friends and that many important changes in your life are forthcoming.

Angel—Protection and happiness are coming your way!

Animals—Animals can be good omens, but it really depends on how they appeared to you in your dream. If they were friendly, you will have a great week or two! If they were angered or vicious, you may experience disappointments instead.

Athletics or sports—If you play sports, this is not a particularly big deal. But if you don't, this dream means you will have some tense moments. Expect a doctor or dentist appointment in the near future.

Baby—This dream can have many different meanings, depending on what the baby looked liked. If it was pretty, the dream means your friends will be loyal and help you if needed. If the baby was ugly, watch out for someone in your social circle who is two-faced.

Barefoot—If you're entirely naked in your dream, you will be very lucky. If only your feet were bare, expect some troubling times.

Basement—Means don't bow to pressure. Stand strong in your beliefs. You could be influenced by others to do some shady things.

Beasts—A lot of adults still dream of scary monsters. They represent problems and delays ahead. However, if you managed to scare the beasts away, the dream means you will overcome any difficulties on your path.

Book—You will have a pleasant, peaceful life.

Boys—This is a good omen. Lucky times are coming!

Brother—If you're a woman, dreaming of your brother means family harmony. If you're a man, this dream foretells of family squabbles.

Bugs—Usually this dream gives you a warning that some of your friends or co-workers could be negative and talking behind your back.

Bus—If you're riding a bus, this dream means you are making progress.

Butterfly—You will be popular and well liked.

Cake—Any kind of dream involving a cake is considered lucky!

Calendar—Your worries are coming to an end.

Chocolate—To dream of chocolate candy means your health will be good.

Christmas—If you dream of this holiday in any month other than December, there will be happy times ahead.

Climbing—You will succeed at whatever you are doing.

Clown—You should seriously think about changing your friends.

Coins—There will be unexpected money coming your way!

Colors—The interpretation of this dream is based on the particular color in it. The colors have different meanings:
  Blue—Means you will experience peace and harmony.
  Pink—Means great success in your love life.
  Green—Expect a nice trip or vacation.
  Purple—There will be a short period of unhappiness.
  Yellow—If you're working hard to accomplish something, expect some setbacks, but you'll succeed.
  Black—Bad omen. There could be danger or unlucky times ahead.
  Brown—You'll have more money soon!
  Red—Good news is coming.

Concert—If you were attending a concert, unexpected good news will come your way.

Cookies—Beware of little arguments over nothing with lovers, friends and family.

Dance—There's a new love on the horizon.

Danger—This is a dream that actually means the reverse. You will overcome any difficulties that lie ahead.

Digging—This means harder work is ahead. You'll need to buckle down in business.

Disguise—If you saw yourself in some sort of costume or disguise, it means you will be part of a devious scheme and be embarrassed because of it.

Dog—Dogs are usually a good omen. But if you see them fighting, it means you and your mate will have many quarrels.

Door—A closed door means you have missed some opportunities. An open door means your hopes, wishes and dreams will come true.

Eagle—An eagle flying means a good job is ahead.

Earrings—In a woman's dream, this is a warning to stay away from gossip.

Elevator—If you are going up, this is good. Circumstances are looking up for you. If the elevator is going down, it means you are on your way down!

Escape—This dream can be interpreted only by looking at the details.

If you are escaping . . .

From an angry animal—you will find that you have untrustworthy friends.

From a fire—you will succeed even though you are worried.

From being held prisoner—you will gain popularity quickly.

If you couldn't escape in your dream—You may be going through a hard time and it will take a while for things to work out.

Eyes—Usually a good omen of pleasant news to come, but . . .

>   *Scary eyes*—Someone is going to deceive you.
>
>   *Animal or beast-like eyes*—There is hidden jealousy around you.
>
>   *Brown eyes*—A new love is on the horizon.
>
>   *Blue eyes*—A new friendship is coming.

Fairy—You will get your heart's desire when you least expect it.

Falling—This is one of the most-common dreams, but it has many meanings. Usually it means there is some sort of fear that you're holding onto. This fear is holding you back from expanding your life.

Fame—To dream of being famous means that you are trying reach a goal that is unrealistic.

Family—Things will turn around in your favor. You will get your way!

Farewell (saying goodbye)—There will be a break-up in a current relationship.

Feathers—You will have a stroke of luck, popularity and happiness.

Fish—If you saw fish swimming, it means money coming to you. Dead fish mean sorrow and disappointments.

Flies—Your friends are jealous of you.

Flowers—You will find lots of things to be happy about. Dead flowers are a warning not to be careless.

Flying—You have great ambition and will reach your goal.

Friends—This is a good omen of happy times ahead.

Future—If you dream of your future, it means there are many unexpected changes coming into your life.

Gate—If the gate is closed, there will be an obstacle in your path that you must overcome. If it is open, you have the go-ahead for a new idea or plan. A locked gate means major obstacles.

Ghost—This dream is warning you not to participate in some upcoming scheme or activity. Resist temptation or pressure from others.

Girl—To dream of a girl means there is some sudden, surprising news.

God—You will have contentment and peace of mind.

Gossip—Don't tell anyone your deepest secrets. They will be found out!

Grandparents—They represent security and protection for you.

Gum—If you were chewing gum, don't trust everyone.

Hallway—A long hallway means a long period of worry. A grand hall indicates wonderful changes.

Handbag or purse—If you lost it, this means you have problems coming your way. If you find a purse, you will overcome any difficulties. Sometimes this dream means that more money is coming to you.

Hero—A new offer is coming with money. There could be a raise in your allowance, or a new job.

History—New and sudden opportunities fall into your lap.

Horse—Riding horses means you are becoming more popular or moving up in the world.

House—An old house means that you will be seeing friends from your past. A new house means more money.

Ice cream—Major success and advantages.

Idol—You will be told a secret. Do not breathe a word of it to anyone!

Jealousy—You will likely be involved in a series of problems regarding your love life and important friendships.

Journey—You will feel as if your whole world is changing.

Ketchup—A new friend of the opposite sex is coming into your life.

Kidnap—If you were kidnapped, you will soon be embarrassed about something. If you kidnapped someone, something could be stolen from you.

Kittens—For women, dreaming of kittens mean a happy love affair, but one that will not last. For a man, there will be many disappointments in his relationships.

Leopard—You may have hidden enemies around you.

Lie—If you dreamed that you told lies, there's trouble ahead because you're acting foolish.

Light—You will feel excited and hopeful about something you gave up on a while ago.

Love – Happiness.

Mansions—If the mansion was elegant, you may experience a change that you do not like. If it was empty, these changes will be to your liking.

Marriage—For single people to dream they are getting married means that they are coming into a relationship that will not last and that they should look elsewhere for love.

Mask—Deceit. People you associate with are not being honest.

Money—If you are receiving money in your dream, this is usually a good omen. Finding money means you will have mixed blessings. Losing money actually means a windfall coming to you.

Mountain—A mountain is the classic "obstacle dream". Simply put, there is something you must get over.

Ocean—A calm ocean means good times for you and your social circle. A stormy ocean means you will need courage to overcome problems in the next few weeks.

Parade—Expect more money to come your way.

Parents—If you dream of Dad, you will have good luck with work or a new job. If your mother showed up in a dream, expect a new love relationship to come into your life.

Pirate—The pirate dream tells you of exciting new ventures. But be cautious of new people; they may not be what they appear to be.

Police—You have security. You are safe.

Race—This is an "obstacle dream". If you win the race, expect good things to come your way. If you lose, it means you have to work harder to accomplish your goals.

Rain—You'll see huge improvements in a current situation.

Rainbow—Say goodbye to your troubles. There will be great happiness.

Rats—You will have trouble because of jealous people. However, white rats mean that you will be protected against negative people.

Rattlesnake—Someone around you is lying, possibly a new love interest.

Road—If the road in your dream is straight, you will have smooth, steady progress over the next few weeks. If it is bumpy or rough, know that you will have to overcome some problems.

Robber—You are in danger of losing your head in love.

Running—You would like to escape from something.

School—You may have a problem with money for a few days. It also means you need to let go of the past and be open to learning new things.

Sister—For a woman to dream of her sister, there may be family troubles ahead. For a man, it means he will feel emotionally secure about himself.

Snake—The snake can warn of lots of troubles, accidents and the danger of being cheated by someone.

Steal—Be more cautious with your money and how you spend it.

Teacher—To dream of a teacher means there will be arguments with authority figures. This is not a good period to argue, and you should try to avoid getting into challenging discussions over the next few weeks.

Teeth—Broken teeth mean a love affair is ending. But . . .
   Getting your teeth pulled—There is a good job coming soon.
   Loose teeth—You may have some untrustworthy friends.
   Nice, white teeth—You will have happiness.

Travel—To take a journey foretells a change in your money or popularity.

Vampire—You could be experiencing a lot of emotional conflict.

Watch—Your friends will help you get ahead in life.

Zodiac—If you had a dream about the signs of the zodiac, you will one day have great success, fame and fortune.

SIXTEEN

Readings and More

We are all psychic and sensitive beings. Everyone has intuitive powers but some people have developed them and use these spiritual gifts more than others do. There are people who are scared of "seeing" things and deny these gifts. Intuition is certainly nothing to be frightened or intimidated by. The more you use it, the more it grows and becomes a natural part of your everyday existence.

What kind of pictures does the word *psychic* conjure up for you? An old gypsy woman with a crystal ball? A wizard? Perhaps you think of Ms. Cleo on the Psychic Hot Line.

Well, psychics, mediums, astrologers and readers come from all walks of life these days. No longer are they found only in dimly lit rooms, with flashing neon signs advertising their craft. Many are holistic health practitioners, nurses, psychologists, teachers and people who have developed a gift and wish to share it. Many teach other people through workshops, books and lectures, how to develop their own skills. The new age field is exploding and becoming more mainstream. Almost everyone has had their palm read or scans the daily horoscopes in newspaper.

Palmists, card readers, astrologers and other new age professionals are setting up private offices, hosting television and radio programs and joining lecture circuits. All are using their intuitive powers, but some use different tools to aid them in receiving messages and forecasting. Because there are so many different types of readings available, I've compiled a list of the most popular ones.

Astrology—The science of astrology uses planetary influences to suggest opportunity and challenging times. An astrology chart is cast for a person based on their birth day, time of birth and city in which they were born. The chart also can suggest basic personality traits of the individual.

Aura—Colors in your energy field.

Candle Readings—Psychic looks into the flames of a burning candle for visions.

Card Reading—A regular deck of playing cards used to predict past, present and future.

Channeling—A psychic goes into a trance-like state and channels other energies or spirits to receive messages. The spirit works through the reader, who passes information on to you.

Clairaudient—The reader hears things. Receives messages from spirit by listening.

Dreams Analysis—Used to interpret dreams.

Graphology—Handwriting analysis. Studies a person's writing to predict personality traits.

Numerology—The study of numbers in a person's name or birth date to predict events and life path.

Palmistry—The study of the lines of the palms.

Past-Life Regression—A regression guides you back to a previous life through the uses of hypnotherapy or meditation. The goal is to see who and what you were in a previous lifetime and to help solve problems or patterns in your current lifetime. You may also be able to discover who you have had a past-life connection with.

Psychic—One who uses their intuition to make predictions. Sometimes they visualize or see events unfolding in their mind's eye. Also known as a *seer*.

Psychomentry—The reader senses vibrations while holding personal items (such as a ring or watch). Through the sense of touch, they will receive psychic impressions.

Seer—Also know as a *psychic*. A person who sees past, present and future through their mind's eye.

Scrying – The reader uses a crystal ball or a plate in which they see images and from which they make predictions.

Tarot Cards—A 78-card deck used to forecast the past, present and future.

Tea Leaf Reading—The leaf formation and images found in a tea cup can predict upcoming events.

How To Find a Good Reader

Since the early 1990s, I have organized psychic fun fairs and expos around the country. I have hired readers of all types to work at these events. I am often asked, "What is the best type of reading to get?" and "Where can I find a good psychic?" These are very important questions and they deserve detailed answers.

HOW DO YOU FIND A GOOD READER?

I suggest getting referrals. If you have a friend or family member who's had their cards or palm read, ask them how they liked the reader and if their predictions proved accurate.

Looking in the phone book or calling a 900-line is risky and can be expensive. A better idea is to attend a psychic fair in your area and ask fairgoers for their opinions of the individual readers.

HERE'S A LIST OF GOOD RULES TO FOLLOW:

1. Ask around. Get referrals.

2. If you call for information, go with your gut feeling. How do you feel about the reader?

3. Never let anyone push you into booking an appointment with them.

4. Avoid 900 lines unless they have a good reputation and you can be connected to a specific psychic who has been recommended. Some have their own extensions. But the cost of call to a 900 line can add up, so be careful.

5. Don't assume that the most-expensive reader is the best. I have been to big-name readers who have charged several hundred

dollars for a session, and absolutely nothing they told me came true. Likewise. I've spent $20 at a fair and the psychic was right on the money.

THINGS TO ASK

1. Ask the reader the fee and also about the specific type of reading you can expect. Also inquire about how long the session will last, what you need to bring to the appointment and if you are allowed to ask questions after the reading is finished.

2. Ask if you can bring a tape recorder or take notes. Some readers do not allow recordings of the sessions. Others welcome it.

3. Don't be afraid to ask the reader to tell you a little bit about their background and experience. For example, how long have they been reading and what do they specialize in? Some readers specialize in specific areas like relationships or health.

WHEN YOU BOOK YOUR APPOINTMENT

1. Be on time. Come with an open mind. Don't be nervous. Many times, seeing a reader is just like going into a counseling session. There really isn't anything spooky about it. But first-timers can be a little intimidated. So relax. Take a few deep breaths.

2. Sit directly in front of the reader, unless you are directed to do otherwise. Don't cross your arms or legs, because this can block the energy between you and the psychic.

3. Don't start talking and asking a lot of questions up front. Let the reader do the talking. See what she or he has to say first. If you are telling them everything about yourself, then you are not

getting a reading. The psychic can be influenced by what you are saying and this may influence the outcome of your reading. As a reader, I like to do what I call a "cold read" first. I prefer to begin without the client asking any questions, allowing me to see what I "pick up". Then I ask for questions toward the end of the session.

4. If a reader is asking you for a lot of information, then you not getting your money's worth. You are giving them information to build on. There is a difference between this and confirming whether the reader is on the right track. A good reader will not ask you, "How old are you? Are you married? Are you in school? What hobbies you do have?" They should be telling you these things!

   Sometimes, a reader will ask you for confirmation to make sure she is on the right track. For example: "I see you are working part time right now, on the weekends at a restaurant. Is this correct?" This time, it would be okay to answer back. It helps the reader to know she is making an accurate connection and then can move on to further predictions.

5. It is not polite to shake your head "No" all of the time, even if the reader is telling you things that you do not agree with or understand at the time. Perhaps she is telling you of things that will happen in the future. Be open to the information, write it down and see what manifests in the future. After all, you are here to see what lies ahead!

6. Have a list of questions. After the reader is finished, she may ask you if you have any. Some, she may have already answered but if not, here's your chance. You can ask now for more details and clarification about something that was already discussed in the reading, too.

OTHER INFORMATION

If you find a good medium, hang on to him. There are a lot of ordinary readers out there, but very few are great! Remember, no
one is 100 % accurate, but you should expect a reader to be at least
80 to 85 % accurate in making predictions. Finding a reader who
"connects" with you is important, too. Your best friend may see a
psychic who she rants and raves about. That psychic may be 90 %
accurate on your friend's predictions but just so-so for you. Shopping for a reader is like shopping for a good pair of shoes. Some fit
just right; others don't!

There are those readers with whom you'll make a personal
connection right away. Others, you'll walk away from wondering,
"What did she really tell me?" Have a little patience, an open mind
and don't give up. Besides referrals, you can find psychics at the
new age fairs, expos and on the Internet.

Don't waste a lot of money trying out different people. You
can get mini readings at fairs for as little as $15. The average read-
ing, depending on the area in which you live, can range from $30
to $90. In larger cities, and with psychics who have appeared on
television and radio, fees may be higher, ranging from $100 to
$600.00

Some people try to "test" the reader. They'll ask, "What did I
have for breakfast today?" or "What is my mother's name?" While
there are some psychics who may be able to answer these questions, you can't reasonably expect a reader to know everything. A
medium receives messages, but not always the ones you expect to
hear.

What You Should Expect from A Reading

1. An average full reading can range anywhere from 20 minutes to an hour. Some readers can give you quite a bit of information in as little as 20 minutes. If you have a lot of issues, you may need more time, so an hour is not unreasonable, especially for an in-depth astrology reading.

2. Your reader should give you details and possible time frames for events to unfold.

3. Besides personality traits and reading the "past", a reader should be able to give you predictions for your future. Some readings are good for 3 to 6 months, others for up to a year. Ask your reader how long your reading is good for.

4. The reader should allow you to ask a few questions

On another note, I want you to know that nothing is written in stone. If you do not like something in your reading, you can change it. Readings can tell us of opportunity times and warn us when to be cautious. If I were to read your cards and tell you that you could get a speeding ticket tomorrow on I-75 and 11 Mile Road, you could change the outcome of that happening. You either won't drive that road tomorrow or you'll be extra cautious. So, remember you can change what is said. You do have control over your own destiny. If I saw that you would have money problems in the next few months, you may decide to take that information and change the outcome of the prediction by not splurging on "extras" or by getting a part-time job.

I do not believe psychics should tell people anything bad, unless the person has a chance to change it. This is one reason "first-timers" are scared to get a reading. They don't want to hear anything negative. I have heard horror stories of psychics telling people they have a dark cloud over their head or a hex on them. Then the so-called advisor wanted the client to give them $400 to burn candles to take the spell away. These are the kind of readers who give the truly gifted and spiritual ones a bad name. These bad apples have caused our new age industry to be looked down upon or looked at with skepticism.

Scam artists as such, they prey on people's emotions and make empty promises. They do exist and there are plenty of them out there. If you encounter such a person, refuse to believe and immediately leave. Do not give them any of your money. I also suggest turning them into the local law enforcement agency. This is another reason why referrals are the way to go when searching for a reader.

A good, honest reader will give you choices. He will give you encouragement and hope. He will be positive and upbeat. You should feel happy and more in control of your destiny after a reading, not frightened. If there is a challenging period approaching, a good reader will tell you how to work around it, deal with it or completely avoid it. You are the only person who controls your fate. A reading is like a flashlight. It can light your path, but ultimately it is *you* who chooses to walk that path or not.

SEVENTEEN

Developing Your Psychic Powers

★ ★ ★ Throughout this book, you've learned a lot about the different new age arts. But one thing we haven't covered yet, is how you can develop your own intuitive abilities and psychic powers.

One of the best ways for beginners to get started is to learn to meditate. You need to clear your mind of any outside thoughts and be quiet and still, inside and out. This takes practice. It can take weeks and months to be able to achieve this state of relaxation. If your mind is cluttered and busy, your subconscious mind cannot work through all of the mess to deliver messages.

Prepare to Meditate

When you first begin to meditate, you should find a private place in your home in which you won't be disturbed. It should be a sacred space. There should be no televisions, radios or computers in the room and you should use it only for meditation. Keep this area clean and clutter-free. Turn off your telephone and answering machine and make sure no one will disturb or interrupt you. If you like, you may have a little shrine or altar in this space. Perhaps you want to display a photo of Jesus or a statue of the Virgin Mary or another spiritual figure. Always take a bath or shower before you meditate, so you are clean. Some people burn incense or candles. Others put crystals and flowers in the room.

POSTURE

It is important that you find a comfortable and proper position in which to meditate. Most people sit upright with their spine straight and erect. You don't want your body to be stiff, only relaxed. You should always be comfortable. If you have a comfy chair, use it. Some people have a small three-legged meditation stool. Others sit on the floor. Remember, I want you to feel comfortable, so use what works for you.

You really shouldn't meditate while lying down, because it's easy to doze off and fall into a deep sleep. Your breathing isn't as controlled either. Breathing is one of the most important tools for creating a positive meditation.

BREATHING

When you breathe during a meditation, it is important for you to concentrate on your breath. The first thing you should do is take a deep, slow breath. Then slowly exhale. Do this several times. Do not try to hold your breath.

> **Note:** Never do anything that makes you feel dizzy or uncomfortable during your meditation. If you get a headache, stop and try to meditate later in the day.

As you inhale, visualize yourself inhaling a beautiful white light, the light of peace. Feel that, with every breath you take in, you are breathing in joy, peace and harmony. As you exhale, breathe out any anxiousness, anger or hurt you have felt earlier in the day or are hanging onto. As you breathe in again, know that you are taking in cosmic energy.

EYES CLOSED?

You probably see pictures of people meditating with their eyes closed. Most people will fall asleep if they keep their eyes closed during a meditation. I suggest that you keep your eyes half open. Perhaps focus your eyes on a pleasing object in your sacred space, such as a flower or a photo.

PREPARING AND FOCUSING ONE'S MIND

The most important part of meditation is to clear your mind. This is also the hardest thing to do. But once you learn to do it, it becomes second nature. You need to calm and empty your mind. Think of nothing, even if it's only for a few moments. Then increase the time to a few minutes, then to 10 or 15 minutes. If it helps, visualize an empty TV screen. See nothing. Expect nothing. Concentrate on this empty screen.

When you feel you have achieved a relaxed or divine state of being, ask your mind some questions. Better yet, see what comes in . . . what thoughts or messages come. Ask your angel or spirit guide to channel messages. If there is anything that doesn't seem right to you, or if you feel negative energy around you, immediately put the white light around your body and refuse to process or validate that thought. Think only divine, good and pure thoughts.

When you're ready to come out of the meditation, come out slowly and become more aware of your breathing. Slowly return to a relaxed, conscious state. You may want to write down some of the messages and thoughts that came to you during the meditation

By learning to meditate, you're opening your higher self to receive messages. Your psychic abilities will grow and you'll be able to connect to a clear channel when you give readings or use your intuitive abilities. Meditation can also help you to relax and reduce stress.

Meditation is a good tool, but there are also other tools to use to expand your psychic abilities. We talked about some of the them in other chapters. Here are a few exercises you can do to open your intuitive mind. The more you do these exercises, the more your abilities will develop and grow.

Development Exercises

MIND READING

Have a friend sit face-to-face with you. Place your hand on his, to feel his energy. Ask him to think of a color. When you first try this technique, you may want to limit the choices. For example, tell him to pick from three colors, such as red, pink and blue. Have him choose a color in his mind, but not tell you the choice. Tell your friend to visualize and think of that color until you tell him to stop.

Concentrate, clear your mind and "feel" the color they have chosen. Silently ask yourself, "What is the color he is thinking of at this very moment?" Choose the very first color that comes to your mind. Don't second-guess the first thought. If you were concentrating correctly, it'll be right on the money.

Continue to use this exercise to test your accuracy. Increase the number of colors to choose from as your accuracy rate grows. Getting 8 out of 10 right answers is great! Getting 6 out of 10 isn't bad. If you only get 2 right, don't be discouraged. You may just need to learn to concentrate more. Go back and work on the meditation and mind-clearing techniques. Try again later!

VISUALIZATION

1. Visualizing the Past—Close your eyes, relax your body and mind and visualize something that has already happened—something you know to be true. For example, see yourself on a recent shopping trip with your friend. Visualize a specific store. Take your time and see all of the details, just like you saw them that day. What did you buy? How much was it? See the sales clerk. See any detail you can remember. Put them in sequence. What you are doing is using a technique called visualization. You can "go back" to that time and place. Your mind will recall what happened. Remembering and being able to "see" the past helps you to develop and strengthen your skills to see the future. Once you have accomplished this, let's move onto the next step, visualizing the present.

2. Visualizing the Present—Close your eyes and visualize someone or a situation you know to be true—something that is occurring right now. Are you at home? Are you in the living room?

Whatever you know for a fact to be happening at this very moment, visualize it. See the details in your mind's eye. This is the easiest of all three steps to do. But take your time. Slow down. See everything around you. Your goal is to get "lost in the moment", the exact moment. Do not think any further ahead than right now. Take a few minutes to do this. Be very aware of your senses and feelings now. Once you've spent several minutes refining this technique you can move on to "seeing your future!"

3. Visualizing The Future—By visualizing the past and present, you are exercising your mind to become more open to see things. It's easy to think of the past and the present. Logically, you know that as your reality. Now, let's take the *big* step in developing your psychic abilities. Let's visualize your future! Clear your mind as you learned in meditation. Pick a subject, a time and place. Visualize your mate if you have one. Your job. Hanging out with your kids. Imagine yourself there. Now, concentrate on how this specific time will be spent. How do you feel? Visualize the setting, the place. See other people around you. You can even ask your mind a question, such as, "What is going to happen tomorrow at work?"

Allow your mind to answer. Sometimes the answer will come even before you finish your question. If this happens, your psychic abilities are turned on! If it doesn't, ask yourself the question and wait for the answer. It will come. Don't second-guess any information that comes through. Even if it seems silly, write it down and don't dismiss it.

Perhaps tomorrow you will see the events unfold. Sometimes they will unfold exactly as you saw them and, other times, there will be subtle similarities, depending on how you interpreted the information. This technique works, but it may take time, practice and patience on your part to develop. Use your notes to confirm or validate what happens.

TELEPATHY

Telepathy. *Tele* reminds me of television or telephone, a form of communication, sending messages across the lines. *Pathy* reminds me of a "path". To me, telepathy is sending and receiving specific messages through a line of energy to a specific destination or person. We are all able to use this gift on some level or another. You can use your mind like a telephone line or turn it on like a TV set and send out your signals.

Let's say you send a loving thought to someone you care about. Your thoughts are like energy. This vibration is sent out into the universe and locates its target. Your recipient will feel this thought and think of you. If you've concentrate really hard, your phone will start ringing and it will be that very person on the line!

How many times have you thought about someone and they've called a few moments later? Telepathy is the ability to receive thoughts sent by others *to you* and *to send* your own messages out as well. Moms are great at telepathy. They can "tune" into their kids and actually feel what's going on. If there's something wrong with her child, a mother will feel it, even from 100 miles away. A mother's intuition can force her to get up in the middle of the night, out of a deep sleep, worrying about her child. Soul mates and those who are deeply in love often each know what the other is thinking, or finish each other's sentences.

One of the best ways to increase and test your psychic power is just to give a reading to someone you don't know very well. Don't be intimidated. Just do it. Ask one of your friends to introduce you to someone you don't know anything about. Sit across from your new acquaintance and just tell him the first thing that comes into your mind. Tell him about his personality, life and any other ideas that may form. Just let it happen. Let your thoughts flow. At this point, don't concentrate on being "right". Just see what comes. Then ask for confirmation when things do arise. Check with your "client" a few months down the road to see if your predictions were accurate.

The Most Important Lesson of All

Trusting your inner voice is the most important thing I can tell you to do. You can work with all of the wonderful tools laid out before you in this book, but unless you trust yourself—your opinion and first thought—then you are not developing your psychic potential.

Always listen to the first answer that comes to mind. If your stomach is upset, if your body reacts to a situation or a person in a certain way, if you feel positive or negative about something, go with it. Your body won't lie. Your senses won't deceive you.

Your abilities are there, ready to be used and developed. You have these special powers just waiting to be put to use. Use them for your highest good and the good of others. If you ever use your abilities to manipulate, hurt or control someone, negative responses will come back to you. Just like a boomerang, whatever you put out, will return.

So cherish these abilities. Use them, not for fun or games, but to create and manifest a most wondrous life for yourself. Your dreams will come true. Don't believe it when you see it. Believe it, then you will see it! Know in your heart, that by using these special powers and tools, anything in life is possible. Go after your heart's desire.

Expect good to come to you. Throw out any negative thoughts. Replace them with higher thinking. May love and light surround you on your spiritual journey!

EIGHTEEN

Traveling Among the Stars

The Best Cities for Your Sun Sign

Are there certain places you visit that you can't get enough of? Are you drawn to specific cities or areas of the country for no logical reason? For some people, a dream vacation would be Las Vegas, amid the glitz and glamour and *cha-ching!* of slot machines. For others, a week-long stay on a quiet, sandy beach is more to their liking.

Your preferences for travel, vacation and even locales in which to live are often tied to your zodiac sign. Over the past several years, I have been doing more relocation readings for clients. I am helping them to find the best places to attract love into their life, financial and job prosperity as well as spiritual growth. I am counseling on specific cities they should stay away from as well.

Some astrologers call these "solar maps". They are based on an individual's birth chart information; taking the day, time and place of birth and finding areas of the world that compliment the individual's chart in different ways. For example, Michigan is an Aquarius state, because its official birthday is January 26, 1837. So people born under the sign of the Water Bearer may feel at home and want to make their living here. Just as there are certain sun signs you relate better to than others, there are towns, cities and countries that work well with your natal chart too. I consistently do love and compatibility charts. So why not pair a person up with a great city?

I did my solar map years ago. I learned I would have major financial success in Phoenix, Arizona. Business would go well in Florida and Oklahoma. There were parts of California that were favorable for spiritual growth. I would have struggles and be challenged in New York City and Montreal. A few years later, I was involved in a business deal in Phoenix that paid off handsomely for several years. I have a large number of clients throughout the entire state of Florida, and my agent is in Los Angeles, California. He is always preaching spirituality to me! I never had a desire to travel to New York City, but did for an recent appearance. I enjoyed my stay but the city didn't hold charm for me the way the Old South does. My chart also showed that I could build a successful business in New Orleans, and in the past several years, I did open a second office there.

There was a concerned client of mine, who has a son who lived in Alaska. He'd been there for 2 years and had had no success. Work was plentiful but he couldn't find any. People were scamming him left and right. He was depressed. His love life was non-existent. His mother was constantly sending him money and begging him to come home. For some reason, he wouldn't budge. He agreed that his luck had run out in Alaska, but he felt a need to stay there. He wasn't going to give up! I did his astrological chart and tied it to the Alaskan city he was living in. It showed that he would always have struggles and hardships there. Money would be scarce for at least 3 years, and there was no woman companion in sight! I also went deeper into my investigation and found that this young man is the type of person who always takes the hard road when he does something. I remembered that he loved the mountains and open air, so I found some other cities that he might like out West that were more astrologically compatible.

I told his mother that Alaska was a test for him. His soul needed to learn some lessons that Alaska had to teach. I figured that when he felt this was accomplished, he would be ready to move. His mom sent him a taped copy of my reading and soon after he decided it was time to move back home.

There are times in my life when I have been drawn to certain cities or places to visit. Ever since I was little, one of my goals has been to go to Paris. I took 4 years of high school French and 2 years in college, yet have never traveled there. Just thinking about going to France, I get all emotional. When I was in St. Martin a few years back, I learned that half of the island is French. I opted to take the tour to the French side. As soon as our bus reached the French border, tears welled up in my eyes. A friend noticed and said I must have had a past life in Paris for the place to affect me so. The same thing happened in New Orleans, a French city no doubt. I feel so drawn there.

I have been to some great cities and islands and yet have no desire to ever go back to some of them. It's not that they are bad places. I had a good time but there was no emotional connection.

Do you feel *deja vu* about a place? Ever visit a city once and feel as if you've been there before? Could you have lived there in a past life? Or perhaps you're picking up an energy that compliments yours. Just as you have a birth chart based on the day you were born, each city and country has a birth date (and chart). The United States is obviously July 4, 1776. New York City is January 1, 1898. Los Angles is a Virgo city, born September 4, 1781. If you've ever uprooted yourself and moved to a specific city just to be there, it must be compatible with your zodiac sign or what your spiritual needs are at the time. Your experience is likely to be a positive one. If the city's chart or sun sign is not compatible, you may feel no link there or any desire to return, even though it's a wonderful town.

In this chapter, we will look at each sun sign and a few cities that are best suited for travel or relocation. If you know your rising sign, read that section too.

ARIES

Aries love adventure. They like fast-moving cities. They get bored easily, so there'll have to be plenty to do if they're going to put down roots. Vacation spots could include amusement parks. They'll be great fun for thrill-seeking Aries. Cedar Point in Sandusky, Ohio, boasts the best roller coasters in the world and may be a good choice for a vacation. Ft. Lauderdale, Florida, with restaurants, shopping and constant parties may keep an Aries' interest too.

Aries cities—San Francisco, California; Nashville, Tennessee; Ft. Lauderdale, Florida

Aries States—There are no states with an Aries' sun sign.

TAURUS

Taurus is an earth sign and therefore comfortable, wide-open spaces may appeal to the Bull. They also enjoy fine dining, so cities known for gourmet dishes will do. A trip to the wine country in California may be good idea, camping in the Smoky Mountains and relaxed locales are what Taurus seeks.

Taurus cities—Honolulu, Hawaii; Lexington, Kentucky; and Greensboro, North Carolina.

Taurus States—Louisiana, Minnesota and Maryland

GEMINI

Location is important if a Gemini is going to move. Finding a good library, museum, theater and music hall are a must for Gemini. They enjoy the social scene. Variety is so important that a city that offers "it all" is probably the best choice for the Twins. And travel, shopping, dining as well as nature would please this fickle sign.

Gemini cities—Houston, Texas; Kansas City, Missouri; Hot Springs, Arkansas' and Flagstaff, Arizona

Gemini states—Kentucky, Tennessee, South Carolina, Wisconsin, Rhode island and West Virginia

CANCER

The moon child loves anything historical or tied to the past. A quaint Victorian village perhaps, a Civil War battlefield or a little old Americana town. Any place by the water will do as well! There has to be an emotional tie to a place for a Cancer to put down roots. Most like to raise a family where they grew up. It's an easy choice!

Cancer cities—Niagara Falls, New York; Richmond, Virginia; Baton Rouge, Louisiana; and Santa Fe, New Mexico

Cancer states—Washington, Oregon and Alaska

LEO

Shop 'til you drop, gambling, glitz and glamour, party and pleasure. These are all things Leos look for when traveling. When it comes to putting down roots, Leos still want to be close to the action. A nice town or city that offers a superb work environment, yet lots of drama would be worth a Leo's consideration.

Leo cities—Miami, Florida; Chicago, Illinois; Boston, Massachusetts; Charleston, South Carolina

Leo States—Hawaii, Colorado and Missouri

VIRGO

Those born under the sign of Virgo prefer to live in areas that are clean, safe and healthy. Work is also a deciding factor in where a Virgo will reside. When it comes to travel, these folks enjoy attending workshops and seminars and visiting spas in resort communities. Sedona Arizona would fill a Virgo's many needs.

Virgo cities—Los Angeles, California; Colorado Springs, Colorado; Rutland, Vermont; St. Augustine, Florida

Virgo states—California

LIBRA

Places of beauty and serenity draw the Libra. They are social butterflies, too, so shopping, dancing and fine dining are a must. Cities with theater and art are appreciated too. As far as settling down, Libras like places that are affluent and pleasing to the eye, with beautiful neighborhoods, parks and culture.

Libra cities—Knoxville, Tennessee; Roswell, New Mexico; Riverside, California

Libra states—There are no states with sun in Libra

SCORPIO

Mystery, power, money and sex all interest a true Scorpio. So this sign will look for a home that has an element of all four. New Orleans is a good example. Any place by the water is also a super idea. Places where money can be made run a close second. As far as travel spots, sexy beaches, exotic locales and foreign cities like Paris and Rome may interest the Scorpio.

Scorpio cities—Denver, Colorado; West Palm Beach, Florida; Fresno, California; St. Louis, Missouri; Newark, New Jersey

Scorpio states—Montana, Nevada, Washington, North and South Dakota, Oklahoma

SAGITTARIUS

The Archer loves to travel. Any foreign city will do! They love adventure and trying new things. Sag never wants to be tied down so they move more often than other zodiac signs. Their love of the great outdoors could take them mountain climbing and hiking throughout the Western states. Many live in culturally diverse areas where there are many people to meet and interesting things to learn.

Sagittarius cities—San Jose, California; Memphis, Tennessee; Beaumont, Texas; Spokane, Washington; Tampa, Florida; San Diego, California

Sagittarius states—Pennsylvania, Illinois, Delaware, Mississippi, New jersey, Alabama

CAPRICORN

Historical and conservative cities are what draw Capricorns. They enjoy the quiet life at home, overlooking trees and earth. But they desire an industrial or corporate city to work in. They want to live in a place that is organized, affluent and has a respect for culture and society. As far as traveling, Capricorn will enjoy cities known for their culinary feasts, designer shopping as well as areas that offer peace and tranquility.

Capricorn cities—New York, New York; Cleveland, Toledo, and Cincinnati, Ohio; Detroit, Michigan; Prescott, Arizona

Capricorn states—Alaska, Texas, Utah, New Mexico, Georgia, Connecticut

AQUARIUS

These folks are freedom lovers. They are also very spiritual. So Sedona, Arizona or Casadaga, Florida may be the perfect places for the Water Bearer to call home. They need to join groups and make friends wherever they go. Traveling to cities that are people friendly is a must; like Orlando, Florida (home of Disney World). The western part of the country is known to draw spiritual and truth seekers so this is also a great place for Aquarius to travel or put down roots.

Aquarius cities—Dallas, Texas; Salem, Oregon; Omaha, Nebraska; Biloxi, Mississippi; Tucson, Arizona; New Orleans, Louisiana; Flint, Michigan

Aquarius states—Arizona, Kansas, Michigan

PISCES

Pisces are fish—fish out of water. Anywhere there's a fresh body of water, you'll find a Pisces type. They also love to escape. Many travel just to get away and don't care where they go. Gambling is a favorite pass-time. Atlantic City, Las Vegas and a few cities in Florida are good choices. As far as building their dream home, warm, lush climates are super with lots of rivers or lakes nearby. Romantic cities are also high on their list.

Pisces cities—St. Petersburg, Florida; Lake Charles, Louisiana; Augusta, Maine; Battle Creek, Michigan; Reno, Nevada; Green Bay, Wisconsin

Pisces states—Florida, Maine, Nebraska, Ohio and Vermont.

NINETEEN

Haunting Experiences

The Ghosts of New Orleans

Many of you who know me personally, know that I am fascinated with the magical mystical city of New Orleans, specifically the *Vieux Carre*, better known as the French Quarter. My love of this unique city drew me to make a second home here, buying residential property in a quaint lower-Quarter neighborhood. Actor Nicholas Cage lives around the corner, among other well known celebrities, who at some point were all tourists and eventually bought a local address to call home. Their experience is no different than the dozens of friends I have made here over the last 12 years, who tell similar stories. They arrive for a visit, fall madly in love with the wrought iron balconies, Creole cuisine, River Road plantations and the hearts of the people who inhabit this old southern city.

Many people born under the sign of Scorpio love this town. New Orleans is a Scorpio type of city, incorporating, mystery, mayhem, sex and the underworld, among other things. The intensity of this town spills out like cool jazz, into the cracks and sidewalks of Bourbon Street. Scorpios love mystery. They enjoy a good ghost story. They are intense psychic people who pick up easily on "energy". I know a lot of Scorpios who live in New Orleans, too. If you are born in late October or in November, or have a heavy influence of Scorpio in your chart, you *need* to visit for a weekend. Walk the streets of the French Quarter. You'll definitely sense something unusual in the air.

Beneath the 18th-century sidewalks and behind the hurricane-shuttered shotgun homes, there is something almost sinister about this old city. It's like a hidden energy that most people don't sense because they are working completely on a conscious level. But those who live here, will tell you there is a much deeper, vulnerable energy that isn't felt anywhere else. It's almost like "good versus evil".

The St. Louis Cathedral, the majestic church that stands in Jackson Square, is next to an alley where duels were fought, murders committed and public hangings were a booming business, centuries ago.

The massive cemeteries, also called Cities of the Dead, are found scattered all over town. Memorials to the victims of the yellow fever epidemic that wiped out most of the city, including entire families, are testament to the pain and suffering of New Orleanians 200 years ago. Descendants of early French settlers, aristocrats, pirates, Cajuns, slaves and ordinary folk fill the plots. Among them are those who died too young. Some with unfinished business. Others who don't know they're dead—spirits who refuse to leave the earth plane. Ghosts who remain in their beloved city.

The Travel Channel calls New Orleans one of the world's most haunted cities. It has done numerous documentaries here. Almost every resident will tell you they have seen a ghost . . . .or at least something that has caused them to become a believer. I'm a believer and I'd like to share a few of my stories with you.

UNCLE LEO

The Olde Victorian Inn

The very first "real" ghost story I've ever heard was that of Uncle Leo, the resident ghost of an 1840s bed and breakfast at 914 N. Rampart Street in the French Quarter. Working as a radio disc jockey for a jazz station in the early 90s, I was sent to the Crescent City to do interviews with local jazz historians, voodoo queens and the like. We stayed at this quaint Inn. The proprietor was a lively, little Gemini lady who loved to tell stories. She could weave a tale like no other!

I arrived at the Inn with my friend Bernie about 10:30 p.m. We were up all night, sitting in the parlor, as Miss P.J. told us the tales of the Inn and its ghost. I must say, I am a scaredy-cat. I frighten easily. Even though I've seen all of the Friday the 13th movies, going down in a basement gives me the chills. I can't sleep when I'm alone in a house either. I'm a wimp when it comes to ghosts.

Leo once owned the Inn. In fact, he lived almost all of his adult life there. Now, Leo still stakes claim to this house, years after his passing in 1977. He has been seen, heard and felt by many a guest as well as the owners for years as his spirit makes its way around the lavishly decorated house and lush tropical garden.

Leo died from health complications due to emphysema. I was

not surprised to learn this one morning after I heard heavy breathing in my room where the office now sits. I heard a raspy sound in my room all night. I thought it might have been the air conditioning unit, but I could differentiate between the two and was a little uneasy. I spoke with P.J. the next morning and she confirmed that Uncle Leo had breathing problems and died of emphysema. I was not alone in experiencing some sort of "spirit-like activity". Others had heard the breathing too. Was this really the ghost of Uncle Leo, or another spirit perhaps? Or was it just our imaginations and a creaky old house?

A gentleman who had stayed in a fancy room upstairs awoke the next morning to tell P.J. of an old man sitting in one of the Victorian chairs in his room. He admitted he had imbibed on Bourbon Street but was not, by any means, "drunk". He saw the man clear as day but when he rubbed his eyes and looked back, the man was gone! This guest described his "visitor" in such perfect detail that P.J. showed him a picture of Uncle Leo, and the man confirmed *that* was his ghost!

Lights go on and off, toilets flush, water faucets run, items disappear, only to mysteriously reappear hours later. A contractor working on the house stored his work tools in the kitchen while he went to lunch. They were no where to be found when he returned hours later. He and the Innkeeper looked high and low and couldn't find them. Finally they located the tools in the garden, sitting on a cement slab that had the name "Leo" carved in it!

A maid was cleaning an upstairs room one morning and the door slammed shut. She couldn't open it and started screaming! The contractor was called and he had to take the door off of its hinges to free the maid. No reason was found for the sticking door. That was blamed on Uncle Leo, too.

Leo is really a harmless ghost. He doesn't show up as often as he did in the early 90s I'm told. I guess he's used to the idea of people enjoying his home! Uncle Leo's picture is hanging in the hallway near the door to the dining area. I tell guests to take a peek so they'll be able to recognize Leo if he makes an unexpected appearance!

Uncle Leo is believed to inhabit his earthly home because he is protecting his property. Rumor has it, the house was swindled out from under his nose. According to owners of the Inn, Uncle Leo had two tenants who swindled him out of the house on his death bed. As Leo lay dying in what now is the dining room, the tenants convinced him to sign over the property to them. It is also alleged that the pair used the home as a drug house and stopped paying rent when Leo fell sick. They didn't do any upkeep and the house was in great disrepair when Leo died. Eventually, upon Leo's passing, his family stepped in and contested the will and won a long battle against the tenants.

Court records show that, in 1979, after lengthy legal wars, Phil Blappert (a relative of Leo's deceased wife Laura) took over the property. But in 1981 the property was donated to Harold Prejean, Leo's brother. Meanwhile, the tenants who allegedly swindled Uncle Leo, were still living in the house and claiming ownership. Only in New Orleans!

On April 29, 1986 the Sheriff came in and seized the property and it went back to Prejean. The tenants were booted out. Prejean sold the property and it became a beautiful B & B in 1989.

It is believed that Leo's soul couldn't rest. He had been taken advantage of and his beloved home turned into a house of ill-repute. Today, he wanders through the hallways and throughout the courtyard, claiming his ownership of the Olde Victorian Inn. He should be pleased now. His home is lovely and well cared for.

I was a regular at the Inn for 10 years, often visiting three or four times a year. One night, after hearing more stories about Uncle Leo, my friend Bernie returned to her room next to mine. She didn't want to turn the hallway light off, because she was a little intimidated by Uncle Leo. I thought I'd play a trick on her. After she was snuggled in her room, I sneaked out into the hallway, shut the main light off, hurried back into my room and locked the door behind me. A few minutes later, Bernie tapped at my door. "Did you shut the light off?" she whispered. (I could tell her voice was shaky). "No, I didn't", I lied. "Oh my God!" Bernie squealed! She flipped the hall light back on and went into her room. I chuckled as I dozed off. A few hours later I awoke out of a deep sleep. A light was shining in my eyes. It was the lamp sitting on my night stand next to the bed. Someone or something had turned it on. Perhaps Uncle Leo! My door was locked, so absolutely no one could have gotten to my lamp switch.

Uncle Leo was playing a trick on me for scaring Bernie! I pulled the covers over my head, my heart was pounding wildly and no, I didn't dare shut the light off!

The next morning I heard Bernie at the breakfast table telling the other guests about the hallway light. I didn't breathe a word of what happened to me. Little did they know, I was the one with the real ghost story to tell!

BOURBON STREET BYGONES

735 Bourbon

Over Memorial Day weekend, my friends asked me to check out a club called 735 Bourbon. It sits smack dab in the middle of the legendary street it was named after. They wanted to see what psychic impressions I could pick up about this place. It was a former brothel that ironically also housed a nursery on the third floor around the turn of the century. There was a private carriage way where gentlemen callers, who wanted to be discreet, could park their horses and buggies

As Keith and I walked in, I was immediately drawn to the back of the club. He said, "Go this way", motioning me upstairs. "No", I argued, "This way. This is where I feel the most energy". I felt drawn to the back of the building. Keith told me there had been slave quarters back there. I walked around and then proceeded upstairs to what now is a ballroom of sorts with a Bourbon Street balcony. I closed my eyes as thoughts and images starting to appear in my mind's eye. Keith kept asking me "What do you see? What do you feel?" I begin to tell him the story of the house.

> *"The front of this house projects an image of gaiety, laughter and fun. I see women in fancy dresses waving to the crowds below on the street. But this house holds dark secrets in the back part, perhaps in the slave quarters, that aren't pleasant. I think someone lost a child or there was a forced abortion. A Creole woman was pregnant with a wealthy young man's child. The man is blonde and well dressed. The woman has caramel colored skin and is very pretty. But she is so sad. So very sad. She had an accident while arguing with her young lover and fell over the balcony and died."*

Keith suggested we go downstairs and talk to the bartender. The bartender knew all about the history of the house. He had seen ghosts and strange things, especially on the second and third floors. He confirmed some of the bits and pieces I had felt. The third floor was indeed a nursery over 100 years ago. The "working girls" kept their babies upstairs and kept their business downstairs. Huge parties were held here. One night a pregnant woman fell from the third floor down to the second. She and the baby died. Now, the ghost of this woman is often seen on the balcony late at night. Her footsteps are heard going back and forth, up and down, the second and third floor staircase. A baby's cry can be heard coming from the closed third floor. But upon the staff's investigation, no one or nothing is found. Legend has it that the ghost is searching for her lost child.

MAMA ROSA'S

I have always believed but never really witnessed any real ghost phenomena until I spent some time in New Orleans. Immediately after the Bourbon Street club incident, I met up with three of my friends and we went to a great little Italian restaurant called Mama Rosa's, a few blocks down from the Olde Victorian Inn. The hallway to the bathroom there, is long, narrow and situated in back of the restaurant. I was waiting impatiently for my friend Sharlotte to "finish up" so I could use the one-hole outhouse. I kept knocking on the door, "Hurry up!", I'd say. I swear she was taking longer on purpose. Then behind me, almost in my ear, I heard a man's raspy voice whisper "LOWER!"

I looked around. The hair stood up on the back of my neck.

"Sharlotte!" I shrieked as I knocked on the door, "Did you say something?" "No" she said as she opened the door. "Your face is white. You look like you've seen a ghost." "I didn't see a ghost", I replied, "but I think I heard one".

We went back to our table and explained to our friends Judy and Sherry what had just happened. The waiter came over and I said, "Listen, I haven't had anything to drink. I'm not weird or anything. But I just heard something back there. Is this place haunted?" "Nope", he replied. "I've been working here for 2 years and there are no ghosts or anything like that here. Maybe you just heard the female impersonator show that's going on upstairs."

I didn't buy it. I knew what I'd heard. However, it was still hard to believe, because things like this just don't happen to me. There was a full moon and an eclipse that night, so I guess anything was possible! About 2 minutes later, the manager came over to our table and introduced herself. The waiter had told her about my experience "There are ghosts here." she said. "This restaurant was built over the very first cemetery in New Orleans". We all gasped! That's what "lower" meant I surmised. If I were to look lower, underground, under this restaurant, we'd find a cemetery . . . among other things! She then invited me to come up to the closed-off second floor to see if I "felt" anything. She warned us that she wasn't going to tell me anything except that she had "experiences" when she worked alone at night. Apparently this area had not been used for years. I agreed, and my friends, who are not professional ghost hunters, but really a bunch of wide-eyed thrill-seekers, assumed they were going too.

We followed the manager up a creaky, long flight of dark stairs. A few small lights were burning and the room at the top of the steps appeared to be a ballroom with a stage. I immediately was drawn to the far right corner, where a dark hallway beckoned me amid long black velvet drapes. I, of course, was first to lead the way. Sherry was behind me. Judy after her and crazy Sharlotte, carrying a 64-ounce frozen piÔa colada in her clammy hands. As I made my way down the hallway, I felt a chill. I moved cautiously. I could feel an energy drawing me in. I stopped for a spilt second in front of a darkened dressing room and peeked in. What I saw startled me! There was a man's face that appeared to be floating against a side wall. He had dark hair and dark eyes and looked about 20 years old. I let out a scream, probably because I was taken by surprise, rather than frightened. (Yeah, right.) Sherry didn't see anything, but when I screamed, she turned and started to run. She tripped over Judy, who was making her getaway, who tripped over Sharlotte, who landed face down, spilling the piÔa colada all over the floor. Some ghost busters *we* were! All this time, the manager was just sitting back, watching calmly. Not a care in the world.

I then directed my attention to the other side of the room and began to "feel for energy". I detected some here and there and, as I was expressing my thoughts, Sherry and Judy let out more screams! My ghost-busting buddies took off, flying down the steps. What happened? Apparently Judy and Sherry both looked back toward the dark hallway they had run from. At the same time, they witnessed a dark silhouette or the figure of a man standing in the light near the stage. Rumor has it that the upstairs was a performance area and the actors and musicians from a bygone era may still be lingering around for a final performance. We weren't sticking around to catch it! When Sharlotte returned home a few days later, her husband asked what was wrong with her arm. She then noticed she had the imprint of a tennis shoe on her forearm. Judy must have stepped down hard on Sharlotte's arm, as she was running from the ghost! We had never laughed so hard!

Here are some true accounts of ghosts that have been investigated by researchers into the paranormal over the years in New Orleans. You can actually visit the sites where the apparitions appear, because many of them are storefronts and businesses now.

JULIE, A NEW ORLEANS LEGEND

A very-popular legend of this enchanting city is the legend of a ghost named Julie. About 200 years ago, many wealthy gentleman and plantation owners enjoyed the custom of taking a mistress. They would establish a home with their family and buy another place for their mistress whom they'd support along with any children they would have together.

There was such a mistress named Julie who lived with her wealthy gentlemen at 732 Royal Street. It is currently the location of the Bottom of the Cup Tearoom in the Quarter. Julie enjoyed a good life, but more than anything in the world, she wanted to become her lover's wife. This was not acceptable in those days, because Julie was a woman of color. It was forbidden by law for a white man to marry a woman of color, back then. She wouldn't let this stop her. Julie begged and pleaded her lover to marry her. He was growing tired of all of the nagging and offered her an ultimatum—one he knew was so ridiculous, that she could never carry it out. It was a freezing, rainy evening in December. He told Julie that if she would spend the entire night on the roof of their home without blankets or clothing on, the next morning he would marry her. If she didn't, she must agree never to bring up the issue of marriage again. He didn't believe she would do this, went out to entertain friends and forgot about the ultimatum.

The night turned into the wee hours of the next morning and he couldn't find Julie when he retired to their bedroom. The door to the attic was open, however; and he felt an icy wind blow through. She had done it! Now he'd have to marry her—or would he? He found Julie huddled by the side of the chimney without a stitch of clothing on. She was dead. She had frozen to death.

The people of New Orleans have stated that every year, usually on the coldest night of December, someone will see Julie on the rooftop of the Bottom of the Cup. She is still waiting to be married, and by morning her ghostly figure fades away. However, at other times throughout the year, Julie has been found in the shop's tea room and it's rumored that she appears anytime her name is mentioned.

MADAME LALAURIE, A GRUESOME TALE

The year was 1834. Socialite Madame Delphine LaLaurie was a well-known figure in New Orleans high society. She was married to a doctor and they lived on the corner of Royal and Governor Nichols Streets in the Quarter. The newspaper of the time, the *New Orleans Bee*, reported the following story.

Madame LaLaurie was getting ready for one of her lavish parties. Her servants were busy preparing for the festivities. A little servant girl was combing Madame's hair and pulled a tangle. Madame LaLaurie flew into a rage and beat the 12-year-old with a bullwhip. The young servant ran out on the balcony, climbed onto the railing and then accidentally fell into the courtyard below. The girl died. Madame was brought into court over the incident, fined a few hundred dollars and let go. News spread of her abusing other servants too, but nothing was done.

On April 10, 1834, a fire broke out at the LaLaurie home. Some historians say the servants started the fire to draw attention to the abuse. The fire department attempted to put out the flames in the kitchen, which was in a separate building from the main house. Servants directed the firemen to a locked room on the third floor. Shrieks and groans could be heard coming from inside the room as the firemen broke down a door. The men started vomiting from the awful stench . . . the stench of death! A number of slaves were chained to walls, some maimed and disfigured. They were victims of Dr. LaLaurie's medical experiments. Many were dead, but some were still breathing. Reports show that the slaves' faces had been altered to look like gargoyles. A man appeared to have had a botched sex-change operation. A once-shackled woman didn't know the firemen had come to rescue her and ran. She thought she was going to be tortured more, and jumped out of the third floor window to her death. That particular window is still sealed today. The newspaper also reported that a woman's skin was peeled off in a circular pattern. The experiment made her look like a human caterpillar. Another had been locked in a cage with all of her joints broken and then reset at weird angles. The woman looked like a human crab.

Law enforcement officials removed the victims and news spread as an angry mob gathered around the LaLaurie home. The LaLauries were able to escape through a carriage way and made their way out of town. Some believe they ran to Paris. Soon after, the building became known as the Haunted House. People heard screams and muffled cries at all hours of the day for weeks after the fire. Some would not walk past the house, fearing the ghosts. For over 40 years, the home stood vacant.

A family moved in one day and had experienced all sorts of strange phenomena. It was reported that dead animals were found in the courtyard and bloody ghosts roamed the stairs in chains. At some point, the place was used as a furniture store. The shopkeeper would arrive in the morning and find feces and blood on the inventory. He moved to a new location. Another man opened "The Haunted Saloon" on the property, but locals refused to patronize the place and the building sat vacant again.

Later, the building was turned into apartments. When the floor boards were replaced in the slave quarters, the bodies of over 50 people were found and determined to have been buried alive! The screams and cries, heard days and weeks after the LaLaurie fire by neighbors, were those of slaves buried alive. Now you can understand why this is considered the most haunted house in the French Quarter!

THE ANDREW JACKSON HOTEL

At 919 Royal Street was once a boys' boarding school. Now it's the quaint Andrew Jackson Hotel. In the 1700s a fire swept through the Quarter and the building was destroyed. Five little boys lost their lives that day. Even though, mostly adults stay at the hotel, guests have repeatedly heard voices of the little boys playing in the courtyard. They'll call the desk clerk in the middle of the night to ask, "Please keep the children quiet!"

JEALOUSY AND MURDER

O Flaherty's Irish Pub is located at 514 Toulouse Street, in the Quarter. But 200 years ago it was the home of Mary Wheaton. Her husband, a Frenchman named Joseph had a mistress named Angelique. This mistress was extremely demanding and in 1810 threatened to tell Joseph's wife about their affair. An angry Joseph threw Angelique off a second floor balcony into the courtyard. He then dug a grave and buried her in the garden, where her body still remains today. But Joseph's crime didn't go unnoticed. A servant child saw the entire incident. Joseph panicked and then took his own life. He hung himself in a room on the third floor. In 1818 Mary died and now all three spirits are said to haunt the pub. The ghostly figure of a woman is often seen overlooking the second floor balcony when music is being played.

MURDER AT THE ROYAL CAFE

At the corner of St. Peters and Royal Streets stands a beautiful building. It was once known as the LaBranche house and was built in 1835. Mr. LaBranche kept a mistress named Melissa on the other side of town. It was not a well-kept secret, because Mrs. LaBranche found out about the whole affair. Her husband was killed in a duel, and shortly after his death, Mrs. LaBranche invited Melissa to the house. It is believed that she drugged the young woman with a drink. The revengeful Mrs. LaBranche dragged Melissa up to the attic and chained her against to wall. When Melissa "came to", she started stomping her feet and making noise to gain attention. Her shoes fell apart, because she was pounding and kicking so hard. No one heard her pleas. Melissa died from the intense heat and dehydration.

Today, Melissa's ghost appears barefoot in the Royal Cafe, now a restaurant. Mrs. LaBranche's ghost is also evident here. Every time the spirit of Melissa attempts to go down beyond the third floor, Mrs. LaBranche's ghost creates some sort of disturbance. Ceiling fans and lights come on. Cold drafts appear and people have reported seeing spirits. Even in death, Mrs. LaBranche refuses to let Melissa go, and is safeguarding the staircase.

Why is New Orleans So Haunted?

I think the reason there are so many ghosts and hauntings in New Orleans is that there is so much history. Buildings are preserved, not torn down in the French Quarter. Some of the houses are over 200 years old. You'll see furniture from the 1700s in antique shops on Chartres and Royal Streets. All of the energy and spirit of people who died suddenly or perhaps at a young age, are still alive. New Orleans experienced hurricanes, war, a yellow fever epidemic and some major fires. Violent death is coupled with strong emotion. Souls continue to search for lost loves and refuse to give up ownership of their plantations. Ghosts still "see" their material possession here because nothing is ever destroyed. It's validation of their prior earthly existence. Their energy will remain alive . . . for whatever reason!

GHOSTS VERSUS SPIRITS

You don't need to visit New Orleans to find ghosts or spirits. Often when I am counseling people, they share with me their own personal "stories". They feel so relieved when I tell them they aren't going crazy. Ghosts actually do exist.

I believe there is a major difference between the spirit of a person and a true ghost. The spirit of someone may appear or try to connect with loved ones or a certain surrounding. They are not here to haunt us. Many times our deceased loved ones may "be around" us in time of need or crisis. They are here to comfort. A ghost however is a different story. Many ghosts refuse to leave a home or give up their attachments. They want to hold on to something or someone they've loved in the past. Some want to haunt their previous residence to scare the "intruders" (new owners) away. Some don't even know they're dead. Others just want to be validated.

Have you seen the movie *The Others,* with Nicole Kidman? I hate to give away the superb ending, for those of you haven't seen it, but Kidman played a ghost who wouldn't accept the fact that she was dead. She believed she was still among the living. It's a fascinating movie.

There are also ghosts who can't move onto the next realm until justice has been served. They have unfinished business. Most of our loved ones pass on to the other side, but for those whose lives have been abruptly cut short, who have been murdered or who committed suicide, the transition to the other side is not always an easy one. There are many souls that remain earthbound and try desperately to communicate with the living.

As I mentioned before, some people whose lives end prematurely, aren't even aware they are dead. These are the disembodied spirits that we consider to be ghosts. In other cases, some spirits recreate the scene of their death again and again in the exact location. This type of haunting is usually created by very strong emotions. While you can hear some ghosts, others can actually be seen. I was working with a client who brought in photos of his local cemetery in which one could actually see lights and a fog-like substance above the tombstones.

Ghosts don't always resemble flowing white sheets. Sometimes you may just see a quick flash of light or a shadowy figure. Other times they leave a draft or chill and create strange "energy" in a room. When someone sees an actual face or body of a ghost, this is called an *apparition*; like the face I saw at Mama Rosa's.

Many spirits just want to be acknowledged rather than to scare you. If you ask a spirit to leave, they will usually disappear if you are firm in your tone of voice and direction. You can tell them to "leave" or to "go into the light".

THE SPIRIT OF A LOVED ONE

The spirit of someone who passes on may linger around for a while, usually right after his death. In most cases, it is to console those left behind. In other cases, it is for unfinished business.

When my father was a young man, his mother died. He could not bring himself to attend the funeral, he was so heartbroken. The evening of her burial, he was upstairs in his room. He heard footsteps coming up the stairs. He recognized intuitively that it was "Ma". He sat upright in bed and waited for her. Her spirit passed by the room. He remembered the incident well 75 years later. He said she was dressed all in white, in a flowing long dress. She passed his room and went down the hallway. He was disappointed that she didn't stop for him, but figured she was going to Pa's room. Then she vanished. My grandma's spirit had come to say goodbye and I believe the farewell was meant for my father, so he could see her one last time. Her presence greatly comforted him.

My friend Jackie has had a spirit attachment that we're still trying to reconcile. She moved to a small town to be with her fiancée, who she later married. His mother had died in the house they lived in, and almost every night, the bed would shake. Jackie's husband wouldn't feel anything or even wake up. But her side of the bed was shaking so hard, that it would wake her up. This happened just as she was dozing off every night. When she moved 2 years later, the spirits followed. By this time, they were really trying to get her attention. She said she felt as if there were two spirits, one woman and a male energy. The bed would jerk so violently that she was frightened. Time and time again, her husband slept through. She even woke him up a couple of times, but then the activity ceased. Jackie thinks it's her mother-in-law, who died of cancer, trying to make contact.

Jackie is quite a good intuitive and perhaps her mother-in-law thinks she is more of an *open vehicle* than her own son. However, Jackie's 2-year-old son acknowledges that the bed moves when he sleeps in it. Jackie has told these spirits to go away time and time again. They don't. One day she had a psychic come into the house and smudge sage around the perimeter of the room and say some prayers. The spirits went away for a few months but have since returned. Now Jackie is dealing with them differently. She tells them she is going to sleep and then completely ignores them. The activity has slowed down immensely. This is a classic example of souls that don't want to leave their loved ones and have a strong need for validation. They attached themselves to the house, but when their loved ones moved, they moved with them.

Sometimes spirits come to warn you of things. An old wives tale that has proven to be true in my case, is that if you hear three knocks on the door and no one is there, someone is going to pass over soon. It happened all of the time when my mother was in her final months. We would hear three knocks, run to the door and no one was there. Sometimes we would hear trash cans rattle too. That was likely a deceased relative coming to tell us that the time was near.

I had another unique experience. It was Christmas, 3 months after my father had passed. I was awakened that morning by the sounds of pots and pans and shuffling footsteps in the kitchen. (When I was a little girl I was often awakened by my dad cooking oatmeal in the kitchen.) I could hear the rattling, and what a noise his spirit was making! I lay quiet and still to enjoy the sounds of my father. This was his way of saying, "Merry Christmas, I am with you today." I wasn't scared at all. I didn't feel a need to run into the kitchen because, if I did, I knew the banging would stop! Eventually it did and I felt as if I had received a wonderful Christmas present.

If you have lost someone, please know that you can still connect with your loved ones, either through your dreams or a meditative state, which is the easiest way for their spirits to connect with you. We are all just energy, and our energy can transcend time and space. It is said that our soul leaves our body when we take our last breath. My friend Cindy was with my mother when she took her last breath. She saw her spirit rise from her body, get up and float through some shuttered kitchen doors. Because she was headed in a westerly direction, she figured Mom was headed to connect with my brother who lived in the western part of the state. Proof, Cindy says, that our spirit never dies.

Sometimes spirits can help us to avoid a crisis or tragedy. I remember a client who was driving up to an intersection. He stopped at a four-way stop, looked both ways and proceeded out into the intersection. All of a sudden, out of nowhere, he heard a loud, booming voice say, "No! Wait!" He stepped on the brakes.

An oncoming truck almost sideswiped him. He claims that the voice was that of a deceased loved one!

Spirits, ghosts, lost souls and the energy of our loved ones can be easily felt by intuitive people, children and paranormal researchers. Discovering them is really the easy part. Deciphering what they want and why they are here, is another story. The history books and archives of New Orleans can tell us a lot about its ghosts. But rely on your own instincts and gut feelings if you feel spirits around you.

The afterlife is certainly a mystery. Yet, many more people are believing in the "other side". Whether it be through a psychic medium like John Edward or through your own meditative state, you do have the ability to connect the past with the present.

TWENTY

How To Live
An Enchanted Life

I hope you have enjoyed my book. I hope my words have stirred something inside of you. My wish is that you find your true destiny. I hope you will learn to work with your energy field and create a healthier lifestyle. I hope you trust your inner self more and believe in soul mates and love. So many of us, myself included, fall into the trap of a regular routine, a daily grind in which we never stop to look around and feel amazed with life anymore. We are existing, not living.

You can't necessarily change old habits and patterns over night but you can do simple, little things each day to increase happiness. You may want to feel "wonder" again, to be excited about life and enthusiastic about each day. Too many of us don't live in the moment and, really, the moment is all we have. You've heard the saying, "Yesterday is the past, tomorrow the future but today is a gift, that's why it's called the present." Be open to receiving and enjoying the present.

We hurry to get through our morning routine, thinking of what we need to do over the coming hours. When we reach that point, we begin worrying about errands we need to run and, later, what we need to cook for dinner and so on and so on. But what about really enjoying the moment?

I learned to enjoy just "being" in New Orleans. About 5years ago, for the first time in my life, I didn't want to be anywhere else. I didn't want the minutes to rush by. I enjoyed exactly what I was doing and where I was. I didn't look forward or backward. At that moment I was content with just "being". Everything seems alive to me in New Orleans. I feel alive. I have no cares in the world.

You don't need to travel clear across the country to live in the moment. You can do it in your own home or community. Create a sacred space or a place in a corner of your room or a special area in the back yard. Drive to the mountains. Pack a picnic for the beach. Take a stroll down an avenue. Whenever you feel lost, find that place and visit it often. When you think about your place, it will give you energy. Here are some other things you can do on daily basis to live an enchanted life:

Believe in Change

First and foremost, believe that you can change anything about your life that you don't like. Too many times, we think we're stuck in a bad situation. Not so. You have the ability to make choices and changes. It's all about taking a risk or a chance. Usually when you stretch out of your comfort zone and take a leap of faith, good things happen.

TAP INTO THE ABUNDANCE OF THE UNIVERSE

Recognize that the universe is abundant and that you are a part of it. We all come from one Source, one Creator, one God. He wants us to be happy and share in the abundance this universe has to offer. You must feel worthy and get in touch with your spiritual side, to tap into this amazing energy!

DEPRESSION

If you're depressed, the best way to shake the blues is to be of service to others. When we offer our help, compassion and love, our problems don't seem so bad. Another hint is to do something creative. When you get creative juices flowing, you'll start to feel alive. Dance, cook, draw, write, sing, make crafts or just visit an art museum or theater. When you welcome art and beauty into your life, it seems so much brighter.

FOOD

Watch what you put into your body! Try to decrease refined sugars and flours. Eat more of God's bountiful harvest: fruits and vegetables. I have always said that God has provided us everything we need in our diet. I feel many of our health problems and food allergies are caused by man-made foods.

GET OUTSIDE

Walk outside. Get off that treadmill and walk with nature. Just being outside helps you feel grounded. Take time to look at the trees, stare at the clouds and breathe in fresh air.

BE KIND TO YOURSELF

Every day, do one thing to make yourself happy. Treat yourself to something delicious or give yourself permission to relax an extra 5 minutes. Sleep in on Saturday morning 'til noon!

BALANCE THE CHAKRAS

Learn about and work with your energy field. Know how to protect it and revive it! Understand what triggers stress and tension and prepare to avoid or completely disarm any negativity.

SPARKLE

Get out your jewelry and wear it. It seems so silly, but you'll get an added boost just by wearing some gemstones or favorite pieces. Why save that pretty ring or necklace for a special occasion? You may never wear it. Each day put on a new piece and let it sparkle!

AFFIRMATIONS

Start your day with a positive thought or affirmation. As you get up in the morning, spend a few moments to visualize how you want your day to materialize. If you're in a bad mood when you wake up, your entire day will be spoiled, unless you change your thought pattern. Need an idea for an affirmation? "This is the best day of my life. Prosperity, happiness and love surround me today and always!" Wow!

PLAY MOZART!

Rather than turning on the boob tube in the evening, put some beautiful music on and get lost in the sounds. Or get rockin' to some of your favorite dance music. Move the coffee table out of the way and dance to your heart's content. It doesn't even seem like exercise, but it is!

READ

Always have a good book to read. Take a few minutes each day to read a few chapters, to get lost and escape into another world. Reading will take your mind off the daily grind.

BATHE

Take a really long bubble bath. We jump in and out of the shower in no time, but truly cleansing ourselves means cleansing our spirit too. When we take time to relax in the tub, we're creating a peaceful atmosphere. Add candles, champagne and lots of bubbles.

WALK IN THE RAIN

The next time it rains, don't run inside for shelter. Grab an umbrella and take a stroll. Smell the rain in the air. Look for rainbows. It's refreshing and exhilarating.

SLOW DOWN AND BREATHE

On a constant run? Allow yourself a few minutes every day to de-stress and breathe. Inhale three long, wonderful breaths and visualize breathing in colors of pink, green and blue. Exhale three long breaths and visualize any stress or problems moving away from you.

BAM!

Buy a cookbook and make a pact with yourself to whip up a new recipe once a week. Don't scrimp on ingredients. Make a gourmet dinner and serve it with candlelight.

NEW PLACES, NEW FACES

Many of us take the same old vacations to the same destinations. Promise yourself that this year you will plan a trip to some place you've never been. It doesn't have to be exotic. It can even be a day trip to a nearby town or perhaps to a state you've never visited. Plan it far enough in advance so you can savor the anticipation of this new adventure.

HUG YOUR DOG

Spend time with your pets and animals. They give us unconditional love and never ask for much in return. Did you ever see someone else acting so devoted just because you fed him or pet his head? Animals are very psychic and can help ease sadness too.

DON'T DO THIS TOO OFTEN!

Make a huge homemade hot fudge sundae with lots of whipped cream, cherries and nuts. Sprinkle crushed Oreos® all over it too. Eat every last bite!

POST-IT

Leave "I love you" notes to everyone in the house. How much work is that? A simple little note can bring a smile to someone's face and spread positive energy throughout your home too.

PRODUCT AND EVENT INFORMATION

In case you're interested in learning more, or ordering reports or calendars that were mentioned in the book, I've included the following information:

Astrology Readings by Maria Shaw are available by phone and are taped. Call 810-631-6887 for an appointment. You must know your birth date, time and place of birth.

The Solar Return Reports are available by mail for $38.95, which includes S&H. You must give your birthday, time and place of birth as well as the location in which you'll be spending your upcoming birthday. Reports vary in length, but are usually around 55 pages. You will receive your exact solar return "sacred moment" time as well as a printed report telling you what to expect over the course of the new year. The report also has examples of how to prepare for one's solar return.

Moon Calendars are available by calling Maria's office, or you can order through her website store: www.MariaShaw.com.

If you're interested in attending Maria's Annual Victorian Enchantment Weekend in New Orleans at the Olde Victorian Inn, call the Inn at 504-522-2446 and ask for Keith or André. The Enchantment Weekend is very popular and is limited to just 12 guests, so please call early with your reservation.

Maria's second book, *Welcome to Our Breakfast Table, The Olde Victorian Inn,* is now available. It includes the history, photos and fascinating stories of the Inn as well as world famous recipes from the Inn's breakfast table. Recipes and post-editorial by Keith and André West-Harrison.

Enchanting Moments, a companion piece to *The Enchanted Soul*, is a meditation CD designed to help relax your body, clear your mind and soothe the soul. Added bonus: Meet Your Angel Guided Meditation.

Also look for Maria's first book, *Heart and Soul, A Karmic Love and Compatibility Guide*. Order by phone or through the website.

For a schedule of Maria's national appearances, see her website. You may also sign up for her free monthly newsletter on the web site: www.MariaShaw.com, or write PO Box 490 Genesee, MI 48437. The office phone number is 810-631-6887.

ABOUT THE AUTHOR

Maria Shaw is an internationally known professional astrologer, who specializes in relationships and affairs of the heart. Her critically acclaimed book, *Heart and Soul* was enjoyed by thousands. It has endeared her to many who are searching for a deeper understanding of the mystries of life. Now, Maria brings us *The Enchanted Soul;* it includes concepts and ideas from her popular workshops that are held all over the country. This Cancer sun sign divides her time between residences in Michigan and New Orleans' historic French Quarter. A former television news anchor and magazine editor, Maria enjoys traveling, shopping and reading. She is married to a stubborn Taurus and has two creative water sign daughters.

Blessings,
Maria Shaw